Best Ever RV Recipes

From the Editors of Trailer Life Books

Affinity Group, Inc.

Best Ever RV Recipes
Trailer Life Books

Group Publisher: Joe Daquino

Associate Publisher: Cindy Halley

Editor: Maxye Henry

Production Director: Christine Bucher

Production Manager: Carol Sankman

Marketing Director: Kim Souza

Direct Mail Manager: Christine Elowitt

Assistant Internet Marketing Manager: Stephanie Lynn

Graphic Artist: Doug Paulin

Cover Design: Brian Burchfield

Interior Design: Robert George/Direct Design

The authors and publishers shall not be liable to any reader/user of this book for any indirect, incidental, or consequential damage, loss or injury allegedly caused, in whole or in part, by relying on information in this book. Neither shall the authors and publishers be held responsible or liable for the use of any materials or methods described in this book.

Copyright © 2006 by TL Enterprises, Inc All rights reserved. Reproduction of this work, in whole or in part, without written permission of the publisher, is prohibited.

Published by Trailer Life Books, TL Enterprises, Inc. Ventura, California.
A wholey owned subsidiary of Affinity Group, Inc.

Printed in the United States of America

Library of Congress Cataloging-in-Publication Data is available upon request.
ISBN 0-934798-78-8

10 9 8 7 6 5 4 3 2 1

www.trailerlifedirectory.com

Contents

Introduction 6

Breakfast and Brunch 7
- Stew's Egg in a Hole 8
- Eye-Opener Smoothie 9
- Tip: Instant Chili Sauce 9
- Peachy Puff 10
- Creamy Philly Scrambled Eggs 11
- Alien Eggs 12
- SPAM & Broccoli Pancakes 13
- Driver-Friendly Breakfast Burritos 14
- Allegheny Al's Banana French Toast Sandwiches 15
- Omelets in a Bag 16
- Breakfast Pizza 17
- Egg and Sausage Casserole 18

Happy Hour Nibbles 19
- Avocado-Lime Cream Dip 20
- BLT Spread 20
- Curried Cheddar Cheese and Chutney Spread 21
- Corn Relish 22
- Shrimp and Crab Dip 22
- Lou's Guacamole 23
- Salsa Olé 24
- Tip: Hot Buttered Popcorn 25
- Maxye's Crispy Maxadillas 26
- Summer Sausage 27
- Tip: Raw Vegetable Crudités 27
- Barbecued Sausage Slices 28
- Allegheny Al's Deep-Fried Sausage 28
- Shrimp in Beer 29
- Sausage Rollups 30
- Cooking on the Engine Block 31
- Lemongrass Shrimp for Two 33
- Watermelon Kickers 34
- Walnut Cluster Snacks 35
- Crab Cocktail with Avocado-Wasabi Mousse 36

Casseroles and One-Dish Meals 37
- Ranch-Style Beans 38
- Beef and Bean Casserole 39
- Tip: Plan Ahead #1 39
- Crock Pot Mexican Fiesta 40
- Crock Pot Enchiladas 41
- Tamale Beef Slow Cook 42
- Green Chile Enchilada Casserole 43
- Tip: Too Hot to Handle 43
- Low-Carb Turkey Fajita Wrap 44
- Bud's Chicken and Dumplings 45
- Tip: Cast-Iron Cooking 45
- Unstuffy Cabbage 46
- Skillet Spaghetti 47
- Basic Impossible Pie 48
- Skillet Chops with Beans 50
- Sausage Jambalaya 50
- Jimmy's Sausage Jambalaya 51
- All-In-One Casserole 52
- Crawfish Pie 53
- Quick and Healthy Poached Haddock 54
- Overnight Tuna Casserole 55
- Tip: Plan Ahead #2 55
- Cheesy Eggplant Parmesan 56
- Broccoli Lasagna Blanca 57
- Potato-Pepper-Spinach Frittata 58

Salads 59
- Orzo Chicken Salad 60
- Tip: Salad Dressings 61
- Chinese Chicken Salad 62
- Curried Chicken Salad 63
- Tomato-Garbanzo Pasta Salad with Salami 64
- Grilled Asparagus and Mushroom Salad 65
- California Summer Fruit Salad 66
- Summer Salad 67
- Tip: Do-It-Yourself Salad Dressings 68
- Pomegranate Jewel Spinach Salad 69
- Cornbread Salad 70

Soups and Stews 71
- White Navy Bean Soup 72
- Quick 'n' Tasty Veggie Soup 72
- Greek Egg & Lemon Soup 73
- Tip: Soup Too Salty? 73

Continued on next page …

Contents (continued)

Classic Onion Soup	74
Tortellini Soup	75
Mom Lack's Salmon Chowder	75
Quick Clam Chowder	76
California Avocado Tortilla Soup	77
Campers' Beef Stew	78
Beef and Vegetable Stew	78
Tadhg's Irish Chili	79
Mike's Firehouse Chili	80
Chili with Zucchini, Sausage and Beans	82

Outdoor Cooking — 83

Miner's Packet	84
Tip: Is My Steak Done Yet?	84
Todd's Best Steak	85
Asian Grill Mammoth Ribs	86
Maui-Wowie BBQ Beef Ribs	87
Tip: Foil-Roasted Barbecued Beef Ribs	87
Beefsteak and Potato Kabobs	88
Campfire Stew	89
Southwestern Popper Beef Burgers	90
Beef Sirloin Kabobs with Roasted Red Pepper Sauce	91
Grilled Rosemary Garlic Tenderloin	92
Grilled Pork Tenderloin with Tomatillo and Onion Salsa	93
Smokin' Succulent Grilled Pork Chops	94
Peachy Baked Dutch-Oven Pork Chops	95
Tip: Sweet Baby Back Ribs	95
2-Mees Baby Back Ribs	96
Bayou Barbecued Ribs	97
Kansas City-Style Pork Back Ribs	98
North Carolina Pulled Pork BBQ Sandwiches	99
Arkansas Slow-Smoked Ham with Bourbon Sauce and Glazed Sweet Potato Packets	100
Easy-Does-It Ribs	101
Grilled Pizza with Proscuitto, Parmesan and Asparagus	102
Greek Lamburger with Cumin Yogurt in Pita Pockets	103
Buffalo Burgers on Foccacia with Pesto and Roasted Peppers	104
Tip: Better Burgers	104
R.C.'s Beer Butt Chicken	105
Spicy Chicken Wings	106
Mahogany Broiled Chicken with Smokey Lime Sweet Potatoes and Cilantro Chimichurri	107
Seafood Stuffed Chicken	109
Chicken Plaintain Fijitas with Mango Salsa	110
Tip: Give It a Rest!	111
Pacific Rim Chicken Burgers with Ginger Mayonnaise	112
Pulled-Turkey Barbecue	113
Tip: Easy-Good BBQ Sauce	113
Goat Cheese-Stuffed Turkey Burgers with Roasted Red Pepper Relish	114
Tip: Skin Deep	115
Deep-Fried Turkey	116
Trashcan Turkey	118
E-Z Salmon	119
Bob Lee's Caramelized Salmon from the Great Northwest	120
Poached Salmon Filet or Tuna Steaks	120
Smoke-Cooked Salmon Steaks with Pineapple-Pecan Salsa	121
Grilled Rainbow Trout Adobo with Roasted Corn Salsa	122
Grilled Stuffed Rocky Mountain Trout with Fresh Corn Cakes	124

Entrées: Meat, Poultry & Seafood — 125

Best Beef Stroganoff	126
Hungarian Goulash	127
Beef Lyonnaise	128
Easy Sloppy Joes	129
Crock Pot Pork Chops	130
Tip: Bring Out the Best	130
Crock Pot Stuffed Pork Chops	131
Jamaican Pork and Vegetables	132

Sizzlin' Italian Sausage with Pasta	133
Tip: How to Avoid Greasy Food	133
Stuffed Spudwich	134
Chicken Santa Fe	135
Chicken Piccata	136
Filipino Chicken Adobo	137
Nacho Chicken Delight	137
Skillet Barbecued Chicken Breasts	138
Chicken Livers in Sherry	138
Pacific Rim Pecan Crusted Turkey Cutlets	138
Oven-Barbecued Turkey	140
Tip: Traditions That Work!	140
Stuffed Sole	141
Linguine with White Clam Sauce	142
Thadd's Shellfish Pasta Mess	143
Allegheny Al's Perch Patties	144
Tip: Freezing Fish	144

Side Dishes 145

Potato Pesto Bake	146
Renie's Cheesy Potatoes and Onions	147
Low-Fat Mashed Potatoes	148
Easy Potato Pancakes	148
Corn Pudding	149
Tip: Easy Applesauce	149
RV Trail Beans	150
Tip: Grilled Vegetables	150
Sweet 'n' Salty Baked Bean Medley	151
Ratatouille Rice	152
Easiest One-Pan Spanish Rice	153
Spinach-Stuffed Tomatoes	154
Grilled Artichokes	155
Asparagus Tapas with Red Pepper Sauce	156
Foil-Roasted Herb Onion Bloom	157
Pineapple Casserole	158
Tip: Roasted Garlic	158

Desserts 159

Chocolate Fondue and Dippers	160
Pots de Crème aú Chocolate	161
Almond-Amaretto Truffles	161
Graham Cracker Pudding	162
Tip: "No" to Burned Bottoms!	162
Chocolate Yogurt Pudding	163
Green Dream Dessert	163
Lemon Panna Cotta with Raspberry-Orange Sauce	164
Light, Lemony and Luscious Dessert	165
Scotcharoos	166
Low-Fat Frozen Treats	166
Armpit Fudge	167
Chocolate-Oatmeal-Peanut Butter No-Bake Cookies	168
Tip: Floor Tile in the Oven?	168
Mini Cheesecakes with Chocolate Curls or Fruit	169
Sandy's Chocolate Cheesecake Muffins	170
Crescent-Roll Cream Cheese Bars	171
Ed's Favorite Melt-in-Your-Mouth Fudge Brownies	172
Jumbo Three-Chip Cookies	173
Peanut-Butter Cookies	174
Chocolate Chess Pie	174
All-American Apricot Lattice Pie	175
Mile-High Cranapple-Rhubarb Pie	176
Tip: Grilled Apples!	176
Handmade Cherry-Almond Pie	177
Old-Fashioned Black Bottom Pie	178
Chocolate Truffle Cream Pie	179
Tip: Peanut-Butter S'more Empanadas	179
Classic Chocolate Mayonnaise Cake	180
Self-Frosting Chocolate Zucchini Cake	181
Black Forest Cobbler	182
Cherry Pineapple Delight	183
Rock-n-Roll Ice Cream	183
Ford's Eggless Cake	184

Dinner for Man's Best Friend 185

Home-Made Dog Food	186

Share Recipes, Tips & Hints 192

Introduction

Part of every camping experience is the camaraderie of sharing meals — sitting around a campfire or enjoying a gathering at your favorite RV park with friends and a glowing barbecue.

Most campers prefer not to spend hours inside an RV, preparing complicated recipes that would take just minutes at home with all the usual conveniences. True, we can take a lot of equipment on the road, but with space and weight limitations, most of us prefer to travel light.

Even if you are a solo traveler, a satisfying meal after a day in the outdoors, maybe while you're watching a stunning sunset, is the perfect way to end the day. And what compares to that first cup of coffee in the morning while the bacon is sizzling and the sun rises over a peaceful woodland scene?

With all of this in mind, we've gathered recipes from across the United States and Canada, contributed and road-tested by Good Sam Club members and other RVers just like you. They are delicious and range from easy to elegant. We've even used icons to make it easy for you to identify dishes that take five ingredients or less, are especially fast to put together or are healthy because they either have fewer calories or are low in fat.

You'll also find lots of helpful hints and tips, quips, quotes and food factoids.

What's your style? Do you like to stop at roadside stands and farmers' markets and improvise your meals? Will freshly caught fish be on your picnic table? Or would you rather plan menus in advance for most of your trips?

Do whatever makes your travels fun and carefree. And we hope this cookbook helps and inspires you!

Many of the components for these recipes can be assembled before you hit the road. You can mix your favorite spice blends or barbecue sauce or measure out quantities of dry ingredients and package them in plastic zipper bags to eliminate taking bulky packages of flour and sugar with you. After your trip, why not take stock and replenish supplies, so you will be ready to take off with a minimum of preparation next time?

We hope you will share some of your favorite recipes and tips for the next edition of ***Best Ever RV Recipes***. In the meantime, happy traveling!

The Editors

Breakfast and Brunch!

Driver-Friendly Breakfast Burritos, page 14

Stew's Egg in a Hole

Stew Oleson, host of *RVtoday*, Ventura, California

1 Serving

Butter

1 slice of bread per person

1 egg per person

According to Stew, there are many names for this breakfast classic, sometimes called *Egg in a Poke, Toad in a Hole, Huevo al Hoyo, One-Eyed Jacks* or *Bum's Rush*.

And it's also an RVer's classic because it's easy and fun to make — little preparation with a huge payoff, and the kids love making it.

You can also have some fun with the end result. Add some salsa and make it a southwestern egg-in-a-hole. Add some avocado and make it a California egg-in-a-hole, etc.

Stew is a purist, so he prefers to tear the hole in the middle of the bread. Some of the fancy cooks out there use a cookie cutter, drinking glass or jar top to cut the hole. Use white, wheat or rye bread, depending on your taste. It's a perfect RVer's breakfast!

After you make the hole, put a dab of butter in the skillet and start a LOW flame. Make sure the butter is completely melted before you put your bread in.

Let the bread take in the butter for about 15 seconds and then crack the egg into the hole. If you want to make this an event, do a one-handed egg-crack and impress the company. Allow the egg time to cook inside the hole before flipping.

Here's where the timing is critical. Do not flip too soon. You know when you have the perfect flip if the cooked side of the bread is a toasty brown. Then put another dab of butter in the skillet and do the other side.

NOTE: You need a good flippin' skillet because you have to make sure to flip the bread at just the right time. Timing is everything when it comes to a good egg-in-a-hole. You flip too early and you have a sloppy yolk; you flip too late and you have burnt bread. You might want to practice a few times before inviting the neighbors over.

Breakfast & Brunch

Eye-Opener Smoothie
Brian Spens, Royal Oak, Michigan

 9

1 Serving

- **1** medium banana, peeled
- Mangos, peaches, strawberries or other fruit, optional
- **⅓** cup buttermilk, whole or skim milk
- **¼** cup yogurt
- Splash vanilla extract
- Few shakes cinnamon
- **½** teaspoon instant coffee
- **3** ice cubes
- Honey, to taste

Combine all ingredients except honey in blender. Add honey while the blender is running so it doesn't settle on the bottom.

Instant Chili Sauce
Lynn Dercks, Quanicassee, Michigan

I like a good old-fashioned chili sauce on my eggs and potatoes. Here is a simple fix for the taste buds when you don't have the real thing: Just add a dash of cinnamon to your favorite chunky salsa for a fabulous instant chili sauce.

Breakfast & Brunch

Peachy Puff

Sandy Lusby, Shediac, New Brunswick

8 Servings

3	tablespoons butter
4	eggs
1	cup milk
½	teaspoon grated lemon rind
1	cup all-purpose flour
2	tablespoons sugar
½	teaspoon salt
4	cups sliced fresh or canned peaches, drained, or your favorite fruit.

Garnishes:

Ground nutmeg

Sifted confectioners' sugar

Whipped cream (optional)

Preheat oven to 425 F.

Divide the butter evenly into bottoms of two 9-inch pie plates. Place pans in oven while preparing batter.

Place eggs, milk and lemon rind in blender. Mix well. (Or use a mixing bowl and a wire whisk.) Add dry ingredients and blend until smooth. Pour batter into hot butter in pie plates, dividing evenly.

Bake at 425 F for 20 minutes or until puffed and golden. Fill immediately with sliced fruit. Sprinkle with nutmeg and confectioner's sugar. Cut into wedges and serve with optional whipped cream.

Recipe can be halved if desired for one puff.

This dish, similar to a Dutch Baby, is perfect for breakfast, brunch or dessert, according to Sandy.

"All happiness depends on a leisurely breakfast."

— *John Gunther*

Breakfast & Brunch

Creamy Philly Scrambled Eggs

Sandy Lusby, Shediac, New Brunswick

2 Servings

- **2 tablespoons chive-and-onion cream cheese**
- **4 eggs**
- **1 teaspoon butter**

Here's another of Sandy's favorites.

Beat cream cheese with wire whisk until creamy. Add eggs and beat until well blended. The mixture will have bits of cream cheese that will melt during the cooking.

Melt the butter in medium-sized non-stick skillet on MEDIUM heat until foamy: pour in egg mixture.

Cook 3-5 minutes, or until eggs are set, stirring occasionally.

Each of the 235 million laying birds in the U.S. produces from 250 to 300 eggs a year.

— *Georgia Egg Commission*

Breakfast & Brunch

Alien Eggs
Stan, Seattle, Washington

1 Serving

- 1 slice cheese
- Non-stick cooking spray
- 1 medium egg
- 1 tablespoon milk
- ½ English muffin, or piece of toast
- 1 dash black pepper, to taste
- 1 dash salt, to taste
- 5 drops hot sauce, to taste (optional)
- 1 small custard cup

"For a cheesier taste add ½ of a cheese slice cut up in small pieces to the mixture along with the trimmed cheese pieces. I love the extra cheese flavor.

"I top mine with hot salsa. You can add just about anything to the mixture — onion, garlic, bacon, ham, chicken, and of course, alligator. Great for breakfast."

Says Stan: "My grandkids think these look like little UFOs. The taste is out of this world!"

Place the cheese slice on a cutting board. Put the custard cup on top of the cheese and trim around the custard cup. The idea is to make the piece of cheese fit in the custard cup.

Spray the inside of the custard cup with cooking spray.

Crack an egg into the custard cup. Add the milk, salt, pepper and hot sauce if desired. Mix with a fork. Place the cheese on top.

Microwave for 30 seconds at a time for a total of 1 minute or until egg mixture is done to your taste. Use potholders to remove the egg cups from the microwave.

Toast the English muffin or bread. This gives the Alien Eggs a chance to cool a little before eating.

Place the muffin on top of the custard cup. Hold the muffin in place as you turn the cup upside down. The egg should fall onto the muffin. If it doesn't, loosen it by running a dull knife around the edges.

Breakfast & Brunch

SPAM and Broccoli Pancakes

Estelle Schmidt, Genesco, Kansas

4 Servings

- 1 (12-oz.) can SPAM Lite
- 1 (10-oz.) package frozen broccoli
- ¼ cup green onion, chopped
- 8 eggs, slightly beaten
- 4 ounces feta cheese
- Small amount of oil

Garnishes:
- 4 ounces feta cheese
- Sour cream
- Fresh chives, chopped
- Bacon bits

Estelle won first place in the National Best SPAM Recipe Competition at the 2004 Kansas State Fair with her recipe.

Grate SPAM and add to broccoli and onion. Beat eggs and add to the mixture.

Pour heaping ¼ cup of mixture in heated skillet with oil for each pancake. Cook until golden brown on each side, turning once.

Sprinkle 1 tablespoon feta cheese on top with 1 teaspoon sour cream. Sprinkle with chives and bacon bits.

Makes 12 four-inch pancakes.

"Never work before breakfast; if you have to work before breakfast, eat your breakfast first."

— *Josh Billings (Henry Wheeler Shaw) (1818-1885)*

Breakfast & Brunch

Driver-Friendly Breakfast Burritos

Lynn Bearden, Brownsboro, Texas

8 Servings

- **1 pound bulk sausage of your choice, crumbled**
- **12 eggs**
- **½ cup grated cheese**
- **1 teaspoon butter**
- **Flour tortillas**

You can substitute bacon for the sausage and add jalapeño or other peppers or hash browns if you like.

In a skillet, brown the sausage and drain off fat. Add eggs to cooked sausage in skillet. Cook, scrambling constantly. When done, remove from heat. Have the cheese and flour tortillas ready.

Heat 3 tortillas at a time by sprinkling with a little water and heating them stacked in the microwave for 35 seconds. Bring them out and assemble on countertop.

Lightly spread butter on each tortilla and place cheese and some of the egg/sausage mixture in the center. Roll up tightly and wrap in foil. Continue this process until you have used all your egg mixture.

Keep refrigerated until ready for breakfast.

To heat: remove foil, place one tortilla in microwave for 45 seconds, wrap with paper towel and you're good to go!

Lynn has a recipe for a great-tasting breakfast to enjoy with milk or coffee as you hit the road. This usually makes about 18 small rolls or 8 large ones, depending on what size tortilla you use. She usually makes this at home the day before leaving on a trip, so a good homemade breakfast is ready to go.

Breakfast & Brunch

Allegheny Al's Banana French Toast Sandwiches

Allegheny Al, Erie, Pennsylvania

1 Serving

Cooking oil spray

2 or 3 eggs

½ **cup milk**

4 **slices of white bread**

2 **bananas, thinly sliced**

Pancake syrup

Mix the eggs and milk, stir well. Heat a pan sprayed with cooking oil on LOW to MEDIUM heat.

Dip each slice of bread in the egg mixture and brown both sides in the heated pan. Place the slice on the plate, cover with banana slices.

Brown another piece of bread and make a sandwich. Add pancake syrup, to taste.

You can add strawberries or other fruit, and sprinkle with powdered sugar!

Al says this adds a great flavor to regular french toast.

Breakfast & Brunch

Omelets in a Bag

Jim and Vicki Cooper, Depoe Bay, Oregon

Serves a Crowd

2 eggs per person

Options:

- **Chopped onion**
- **Grated cheese**
- **Cooked crumbled bacon**
- **Ham**
- **Green pepper**
- **Or other additions of your choice**

Equipment:

- **Pint-size resealable freezer bags**
- **Pan of boiling water**
- **Tongs**

Crack 2 eggs per person in a bowl, mix and set aside.

In each bag, put whatever each person wants in their omelet, such as chopped onion, grated cheese, cooked crumbled bacon, ham, green pepper, etc.

Scoop 1 cup of egg into each bag and seal well. Drop into large pan of boiling water for 20 minutes. Remove with tongs and slide the omelet onto your plate or onto bread or rolls to make a sandwich. Throw the bag away — no mess and you have a perfect omelet.

Jim and Vicki say this is great for crowds. Have each person write their name on the bag with a marker and keep track of their time to claim their omelet. You can cook several at once in a large pan. It's very important to use heavy-duty bags or they might break, and bags no larger than pint-size.

Breakfast & Brunch

Breakfast Pizza

Philip Porter, Detroit, Michigan

6-8 Servings

- 1 (12-oz.) package bulk pork sausage
- 1 (8-oz.) can refrigerated crescent rolls
- 1 cup frozen, loose-pack shredded hash-brown potatoes
- ½ cup (2 oz.) shredded sharp cheddar cheese
- 3 eggs
- ½ teaspoon salt
- ⅛ teaspoon pepper
- 3 tablespoons milk
- 2 tablespoons grated parmesan cheese

Try this pizza with Swiss or jack cheese in place of cheddar.

Heat oven to 375 F.

Crumble sausage into medium skillet. Cook over MEDIUM-HIGH heat until browned and no longer pink, stirring frequently. Drain.

Separate crescent roll dough into 4 rectangles. Place in ungreased 13x9-inch pan. Press over bottom and ½ inch up sides to form crust; firmly press perforations and edges to seal.

Spoon sausage evenly over crust. Sprinkle with potatoes and cheese.

Beat eggs in medium bowl. Add all remaining ingredients; mix well. Pour over cheese in crust.

Bake at 375 F for 18 to 23 minutes or until center is set and edges are deep golden brown. If desired, serve with salsa.

"I went to a restaurant that serves 'breakfast at any time.' So I ordered French Toast during the Renaissance."

— Steven Wright

Breakfast & Brunch

Egg and Sausage Casserole

Julie Savoy, St. Amant, Louisiana

6 Servings

- 6 large eggs
- 1 cup whole milk
- 1 ½ cups biscuit mix
- ½ pound cooked, crumbled sausage and/or 1 cup crumbled bacon
- 2 cups grated cheddar cheese
- Salt and pepper to taste
- ¼ cup finely chopped green onions (optional)

Preheat oven to 350 F.

In a large bowl, break eggs and add milk. Blend well. Add remaining ingredients, mix and pour into a greased 9x13x2-inch pan.

Bake about 40 minutes (or until eggs are set).

Egg production in the United States totaled 89.1 billion eggs in 2004 and all eggs averaged 71.4 cents per dozen.

— *U.S. Poultry & Egg Association*

Happy Hour Nibbles!

Appetizers and Dips

Avocado-Lime Cream Dip
Sandy Lusby, Shediac, New Brunswick

2 Servings

- 1 ripe avocado
- 1 tablespoon lime juice, freshly squeezed
- ½ teaspoon hot-pepper sauce
- 1 clove garlic

This can be served as is on corn chips or crackers, or topped with shrimp, sliced chilies or cherry tomatoes. If you don't have a food processor handy, use a fork — the dip might not be quite as smooth, but just as tasty.

Peel and dice avocado. Combine all ingredients in a food processor and puree until smooth. Cover and chill until serving.

BLT Spread
Betty Moorman, Boone, Iowa

1 ½ Cups

- 5-8 slices bacon, cooked crisp and crumbled
- 1 cup sour cream
- 1 cup mayonnaise
- 3 plum tomatoes, seeded and chopped fine

Combine bacon, sour cream, mayonnaise and tomatoes. Stir until blended. Cover and refrigerate 1 hour to blend flavors. Serve with snack crackers.

If you want to be fancy, hollow out a large tomato and put the spread inside. Great to serve at a cocktail hour or a party of any kind, says Betty.

Curried Cheddar Cheese and Chutney Spread

Honor Spens, Rancho Santa Margarita, California

4 ½ Cups

- 2 (8-oz.) packages cream cheese at room temperature
- 2 teaspoons curry powder
- 2 (8-oz.) packages shredded sharp cheddar cheese
- ¼ cup chopped green onions
- ¼ cup port wine
- ¼ teaspoon salt or to taste
- ½ cup mango chutney

Garnish:
- Finely chopped green onions
- Parsley sprigs (optional)

Curry powder and mango chutney give this spread a sophisticated touch.

Hint: Microwave the cream cheese on DEFROST setting for a minute or two to soften.

Mix cream cheese and curry powder until cheese is light and curry is well blended. Add half of shredded cheddar and blend well. Add remaining cheddar, green onion, port and salt; blend until smooth.

Line a 5-cup dish or bowl with lightweight foil or plastic wrap, pressing foil tightly against sides of dish. Lightly spray foil with non-stick vegetable cooking spray. Spoon cheese mixture firmly into prepared dish. Cover and refrigerate 4-6 hours or overnight.

To serve, turn dish upside down on serving plate, Remove foil. Spread some chutney on top and serve remaining chutney on the side. Garnish with chopped green onions and parsley. Serve with assorted crackers.

*Dip is a very widespread food;
forms of it are eaten all over the world.*

— *en.wikipedia.org*

Happy Hour Nibbles — DIPS

Corn Relish
Al Barnett, Pittsburg, Texas

6 Cups

- 1 (4-oz.) can chopped green chilies
- 2 (11-oz.) cans corn with red and green peppers
- 2 cups shredded cheddar cheese
- ¾ cup mayonnaise
- ¾ cup sour cream
- 2 tablespoons chopped green onion (green part only)
- Dash cumin
- Fresh or canned jalapeños, chopped, to taste (optional)

Al serves this relish with tortilla or corn chips.

Mix all ingredients together.

Shrimp and Crab Dip
Chuck Campbell, *Trailer Life* and *MotorHome* columnist, Thousand Oaks, California

4 Cups

- 1 pint sour cream
- 1 (8-oz.) tub cream cheese, preferably whipped
- 1 (.7-oz.) packet dry salad-dressing mix
- Lemon juice
- 1 (7-oz.) can small shrimp, drained well
- 1 (7-oz.) can crabmeat

Blend sour cream and cream cheese in mixing bowl. Add dressing mix, a splash of lemon juice, and blend further until relatively smooth. Fold in shrimp and crabmeat. Transfer to lidded container, and let stand in refrigerator for several hours before serving to allow spices and flavors to blend.

Serve with ruffled potato chips, scoops or your favorite crisp bread sticks or crackers.

Happy Hour Nibbles — DIPS

Lou's Guacamole
Lou Henry, Newbury Park, California

23

6 Cups

- 6 soft-ripe avocados
- 3 tomatoes, rough-chopped
- 4 cloves garlic, minced
- 1 large onion, chopped
- ½ cup chopped fresh cilantro
-   Juice of 1 large lemon or 2 limes
-   Several dashes hot-pepper sauce
-   Salt to taste

Guacamole should be chunky, so don't mash the avocados, says Lou. Serve with fresh tortilla chips.

Mix (do not mash) just until combined.

There are over 500 avocado varieties grown around the world.

— *Avocado Central*

Happy Hour Nibbles — DIPS

Salsa Olé

Jim Milton, Sun City, Arizona

4 Cups

- 3 (14 ½-oz.) cans tomatoes, 2 diced small and 1 pureed
- 5 fresh jalapeño peppers, seeded and minced (or leave seeds in for hotter flavor)
- 1 tablespoon garlic powder
- 1 ½ teaspoons dried or 1 teaspoon fresh cilantro
- 1 ½ teaspoons vegetable supreme seasoning
- 1 teaspoon dried or fresh parsley flakes
- 1 teaspoon salt, or to taste
- 1 teaspoon oregano leaves
- 1 teaspoon sugar, or to taste
- ¼ teaspoon leaf marjoram

Jim suggests refrigerating overnight to make the flavors come together. Goes great with chips or as a garnish to your meal.

Mix the items together and refrigerate overnight.

"Bear in mind that you should conduct yourself in life as at a feast."
— *Epictetus (55 AD - 135 AD)*

Happy Hour Nibbles — DIPS

Ummm... Hot Buttered Popcorn!

For each ½ cup of unpopped popcorn kernels, melt 3 tablespoons of butter and add one of the following combinations, then pour over the popped corn:

- **1 teaspoon herb-seasoned salt blend of your choice**
- **2 minced garlic cloves and 1 tablespoon fresh (1 teaspoon dried) rosemary, thyme or dill**
- **½ teaspoon pepper; toss with popped corn and then add ½ cup grated parmesan cheese**
- **Prepared Cajun seasoning, or make your own with 1 teaspoon red pepper flakes, 1 tablespoon fresh (1 teaspoon dried) thyme, ¾ teaspoon liquid pepper seasoning, ½ teaspoon garlic powder, ½ teaspoon paprika and ¼ teaspoon onion powder**

Happy Hour Nibbles — POPCORN

Maxye's Crispy Maxadillas

Maxye Henry, Newbury Park, California

4 Servings

	Canola oil
1	large flour tortilla
1	(14 ½-oz.) can refried beans, with or without jalapeños
½	cup crumbled and browned ground beef, chorizo or other sausage
½	cup shredded jack cheese
½	cup sliced ripe olives

Garnishes:

    Guacamole

    Sour cream

A friend dubbed this the "Maxadilla" — a play on Maxye's name. Vary the ingredients to make it an appetizer, side dish or entrée.

Fry the tortillas in canola oil to cover. Allow them to form bubbles. If your pan is slightly smaller than the circumference of the tortillas, they will form an upturned rim that will help keep the fillings contained.

Turn them, but only let them brown on one side; the flip side should be lighter in color – it will finish browning when you toast it under the broiler. Drain well. (This step can be done in advance, but you don't want the tortillas to lose their crunch.)

Top the lighter side of each fried tortilla with strips of beans and browned meat, wagon-wheel style. Then sprinkle with cheese and top with ripe olives. Heat under a 400 F broiler just until the cheese has melted – watch carefully so the tortilla doesn't char.

Top with garnishes or serve them on the side so your guests can help themselves. Tear the Maxadilla into irregular wedges – this is definitely finger food!

Happy Hour Nibbles — HOT

Summer Sausage
Wanda Watson, Spicewood, Texas

8 Servings

- 2 pounds extra-lean ground beef
- 2 japeleño peppers, finely chopped
- 1 cup cold water
- 2 tablespoons meat tenderizer
- 2 teaspoons coarse pepper or peppercorns
- 1 ½ teaspoons liquid smoke
- ½ teaspoon onion powder
- ½ teaspoon garlic powder

Wanda says: "Most people would enjoy summer sausage for a quick bite on the road or between meals — except for the fat. Try this low-fat recipe."

Mix all ingredients together. Make into logs, wrap in aluminum foil and place in refrigerator for 24 hours. Take out of foil and bake for 1 to 1 ½ hours in 300 F oven. Cool and serve.

Sausage is one of the oldest forms of processed food, having been mentioned in Homer's Odyssey as far back as the 9th Century B.C.

— National Hot Dog & Sausage Council

Find Fresh Veggies While on the Road!

Farmer's markets and roadside stands are great places to buy fresh, seasonal vegetables. Create a tray of crudites (fancy for raw veggies) instead of calorie-loaded chips, and serve with flavored olive oil or any other dip for a healthier appetizer.

Happy Hour Nibbles — HOT

Barbecued Sausage Slices

Deana O'Hanley, Springhill, Nova Scotia

12-16 Pieces

1   **(8-oz.) package sliced pepperoni or salami**

     Favorite barbecue sauce (optional)

This is a little snack Deana cooks up quickly to buy time till the actual meal is ready.

Heat the barbecue grill and place the sliced sausage in a single layer on the rack. Watch closely and turn frequently, being careful not to lose the slices between the grates. Cook until desired crispness. Brush with sauce if desired. Remove to serving plate and dip in additional barbecue sauce.

Allegheny Al's Deep-Fried Sausage

Allegheny Al, Erie, Pennsylvania

12-16 Pieces

1   **ring smoked sausage, any flavor**

     All-purpose flour

1   **egg mixed with 1 tablespoon milk**

     Cracker crumbs or other favorite coating

     Oil for deep frying

These are tasty bites to serve with assorted mustards and beer.

Remove casing and cut the sausage into 1 or 1 ½-inch rings. Place a toothpick in each ring.

Dip each ring into flour, then egg wash, then crumbs or coating. Remember: Dry – Wet – Dry.

Heat enough oil in a deep fryer to float the sausage pieces. Cook until golden brown, then remove and drain on paper towels.

Happy Hour Nibbles — HOT

Shrimp in Beer

Bill Graves, *Trailer Park* columnist, Rancho Palos Verdes, California

4 Servings

- 1 **pound of whole shrimp in the shell**
- 3 **tablespoons mustard powder**
- 1 **6-pack of beer**

Bill cautions that this is best done on a grill outside unless you really like the smell of hot beer.

In a large pot, pour the beer and bring to a boil. Add mustard and shrimp; when the beer returns to the boil, drain and serve.

"My grandmother was a very tough woman. She buried three husbands and two of them were just napping."

— *Rita Rudner*

Happy Hour Nibbles — HOT

Sausage Rollups

Steve Boilan, Ventura, California

48 Pieces

- 2 (8-oz.) cans refrigerated crescent dinner rolls
- 48 cocktail-size smoked link sausages or 8 hot dogs cut in 6 pieces each

The ever popular pigs-in-a-blanket never go out of style! Serve warm with assorted deli mustards or barbecue sauces for dipping.

Heat oven to 375 F. Unroll both cans of rolls; separate into 16 triangles. Cut each triangle lengthwise into 3 narrow triangles. Place one sausage on shortest side of each triangle. Roll up to opposite point. Place rolls, point side down, on two ungreased cookie sheets.

Bake 12-15 minutes or until golden brown, switching position of cookie sheets halfway through baking. Immediately remove from cookie sheets.

"The ultimate aim of civility and good manners is to please: to please one's guest or to please one's host. To this end one uses the rules laid down by tradition: of welcome, generosity, affability, cheerfulness and consideration for others."

— *Claudia Roden*

Happy Hour Nibbles — HOT

Cooking on the Engine Block
The Surreal Gourmet, Bob Blumer

Bob explains:

1) In preparation for your first engine-cooked meal, you must first locate the engine's hottest areas. Do this after any long drive by turning off the engine and letting the vehicle sit for 15 minutes. Then lift up the hood and quickly tap the various components.

   On most vehicles, the hottest area is the exhaust manifold cover, but most engines have additional nooks and crannies that will generate enough heat to slow cook your freeway fare. Stay clear of areas near any moving parts, such as the accelerator linkage, belts or fans, and don't block any air intakes.

2) Before attempting any complex recipes, get to know your engine. The sensible way (relatively speaking) to take advantage of the oven under your hood is to cook small portions of lightly textured foods. For this reason, fish is the perfect road chow.

   When you're ready to cook: Lay out three equal sized sheets of aluminum foil, one on top of the other. Proceed as if they were a single sheet. Grease the top sheet with a small amount of butter or olive oil

Continued on next page ...

Happy Hour Nibbles — HOT

Cooking on the Engine Block

Continued from previous page

to avoid stickage. Wrap ingredients in foil and seal securely by folding seams to create an airtight package.

Before placing food on the engine, loosely roll up a six-inch ball of foil, and set it on the sweet spot of your engine. Then close the hood. Immediately re-open it and use the squashed ball to determine the amount of clearance space between the engine block and the hood.

Place food on the pre-determined sweet spot, and secure it by placing a ball of foil on top that is equal to the clearance space less the pouch size. If necessary, hold the pouch in place with additional aluminum foil bracing. Make, model, speed, outside temperature, food density and placement will all affect cooking time.

Most small packets of food should cook in 1 – 2 hours. To insure that you have fingers left to lick at the end of the meal, always turn off the engine before loading, unloading or testing for doneness.

"To the old saying that man built the house but woman made of it a 'home' might be added the modern supplement that woman accepted cooking as a chore but man has made of it a recreation."

— Emily Post

Happy Hour Nibbles — HOT

Lemongrass Shrimp for Two

Bob Blumer, The Surreal Gourmet, *Highways* columnist and Food Network TV show host, from his book, *Off the Eaten Path*

2 Servings

- ½ pound medium-sized shrimp, shelled and deveined
- 1 fresh lemongrass shoot, bottom 2 inches only, sliced finely
- 1 ½ tablespoons freshly squeezed lime juice
- ¼ teaspoon salt
- 1 pinch cayenne pepper
- 2 sprigs of fresh mint (optional)
- 3 12x12-inch sheets of aluminum foil

Layer all three sheets of aluminum foil on top of each other and fold up the edges. Sprinkle lemongrass around the center. Place shrimp on top and drizzle with lime juice. Sprinkle with salt and cayenne. Top with the mint, and seal foil package.

Place on engine and cook for approximately 50 miles. (It's not necessary to turn the package.)

Open package and serve immediately. (Don't eat the lemongrass.) If lemongrass is unavailable, it may be replaced with 1 tablespoon of fresh ginger root, sliced finely.

Happy Hour Nibbles — HOT

Watermelon Kickers

Lon S. (Steve) Aucker, Albuquerque, New Mexico

4 Servings

- 1 cup fresh lime juice
- 1 tablespoon tequila
- 1 teaspoon salt
- 1 large dash bottled hot pepper sauce
- 5 cups seeded, cubed or balled watermelon

Just let your imagine soar; this can include all kinds of fruit for a kicky mélange, says Steve.

Combine everything but the fruit in a bowl suitable for dipping. For a foursome, place the dipping bowl in the center of a platter or large round, flat plate. Arrange watermelon chunks around the dipping bowl. Insert toothpicks or short bar spears in the cubed or balled fruit.

For a large group, use the bottom half of the watermelon rind as a bowl. Slice a flat spot on the bottom. Spike the edges if you like. Make double or triple the sauce, commensurate with the quantity of fruit. Place the bowl of sauce in the center of the watermelon rind bowl and surround with fruit. Place the toothpicks or spears nearby.

Happy Hour Nibbles — COLD

Walnut Cluster Snacks

American Heart Association's Simple Solutions, CA Walnut Commission

16 Servings

	Vegetable oil spray
3	cups quick-cooking oats
½	cup oat bran
¾	cup coarsely chopped walnuts
	White of 1 egg
¾	cup apricot nectar
½	cup maple syrup
2	teaspoons walnut oil
1	teaspoon vanilla extract
1	(9-oz.) package dried figs, quartered (about 1 ½ cups)
1	(6-oz.) package dried cranberries (about 1 ⅓ cups)

Preheat oven to 325 F. Lightly spray a 13x9x2-inch baking pan with vegetable oil spray. In a large bowl, stir together the oats, oat bran and walnuts.

In a medium bowl, beat the egg white until frothy. Stir in the apricot nectar, maple syrup, walnut oil and vanilla. Pour over the oat mixture, stirring until moistened. Press the mixture into the prepared pan.

Bake, uncovered, for 45 minutes. Put the pan on a cooling rack and let cool for 10 minutes. Break up the mixture into small pieces or clusters. Return the clusters to the pan. Bake for 10 minutes. Put the pan on a cooling rack. Stir in the figs and cranberries. Cool thoroughly.

Store in an airtight container. To serve, put ½-cup portions into snack-size bags. Mixture will keep in airtight containers up to 1 week. (Freezing is not recommended.)

Take a hike! Clusters of crunchy oats and walnuts baked with tender dried fruit make a great heart-healthy snack on the go.

Happy Hour Nibbles — COLD

Crab Cocktail with *Avocado-Wasabi Mousse*

California Avocado Commission

6 Servings

- 1 ½ cups cooked crabmeat
- ⅛ cup rice vinegar
- ⅛ cup thinly sliced chives
- 5 avocados, diced (2 ½ pounds or 5 cups)
- 1 tablespoon wasabi paste (Japanese horseradish), or to taste
- 1 tablespoon hot pepper sauce (or to taste)
- ½ tablespoon salt
- ¾ cup heavy cream
- 1 ½ cups salsa fresca

Garnishes:

- 12 deep-fried taro chips
- 6 green onions, cut into 2 inch lengths
- Cilantro sprigs
- Diced avocado

Your friends will know that you think they're special when you serve up this elegant first course.

Combine crab, vinegar and chives, reserve. Prepare mousse, reserve.

Avocado-Wasabi Mousse: Just before serving, puree avocados until smooth with wasabi paste, hot pepper sauce, and salt; reserve. Whip ¾ cup cream; fold into reserved avocado mixture. Yield: 3 cups.

Just before serving, scoop ¼ cup avocado-wasabi mousse into each of 6 martini glasses. Top each with ¼ cup salsa fresca. Scoop ¼ cup reserved crab mixture on top of salsa. Garnish with 2 taro chips, green onion, cilantro and diced avocado.

Happy Hour Nibbles — COLD

Casseroles and One-Dish Meals!

Cheesy Eggplant Parmesan, page 56

Ranch-Style Beans

Julie Savoy, St. Amant, Louisiana

12 Servings

- 1 ½ to 2 pounds lean ground beef
- 1 cup chopped celery
- 1 cup chopped onion
- 1 cup chopped green onions
- 1 small green bell pepper, chopped
- 2 cloves garlic, chopped
- 3 (15-oz.) cans ranch-style beans
- 2 (10-½-oz.) cans tomato soup
- ½ cup barbecue sauce
- ½ cup brown sugar
- 1 or 2 chopped jalapeño peppers
- Salt and pepper, to taste

Garnish:
- 2 cups shredded cheddar cheese

Brown the meat in a heavy dutch oven. Add celery, onions, bell peppers, green onions and garlic and cook for 20 minutes. Add beans, soup, barbecue sauce, brown sugar, jalapeños, salt and pepper. Simmer for about one hour.

Serve with cheese sprinkled on top.

Julie's great potluck dish is good with barbecued or grilled foods. Longer simmering enhances the flavor. It can be made a day ahead of time or frozen for future use.

"When I was born I was so surprised I didn't talk for a year and a half."

— *Gracie Allen*

Casseroles and One-Dish Meals

Beef and Bean Casserole
Tom Caylor, Ladson, South Carolina

4 Servings

- 1 **pound ground beef**
- 1 **(15-oz.) can pork and beans**
- ½ **cup brown sugar**
- ½ **medium or 1 small onion, chopped**
- 1 **tablespoon garlic powder**
- 1 **tablespoon salt**

The brown sugar makes Tom's dish extra tasty.

Brown the ground beef in a pan and drain. Mix all the ingredients together in a 3-quart casserole dish. Cover with aluminum foil and bake at 350 F for 45 minutes; uncover and stir before serving.

Plan Ahead #1
Phyllis Powell, Roseburg, Oregon

My husband and I have been camping for almost 50 years, first in a tent, then a camper and now a lovely trailer. I always plan my meals before we leave. I put the dry ingredients for each recipe in plastic zipper bags and label them. This way I do not have to take bags of flour, sugar, cornstarch, etc. in the trailer and when I get home I don't have to unload them and bring them back into the house.

Casseroles and One-Dish Meals

Crock Pot Mexican Fiesta

Chris Behrens, Dover, Delaware

6 Servings

- 1 (16-oz.) bag white corn tortilla chips
- 1 pound lean ground beef
- 1 (14-oz.) can ranch-style beans, undrained
- 1 (10 ½-oz.) can cream of mushroom soup
- 1 (10 ½-oz.) can cream of chicken soup
- 1 (10 ½-oz.) can mild tomatoes and green chilies
- 2 teaspoons chili powder
- ½ cup chopped onion (optional)
- 3 cups grated cheddar cheese

Here's an easy layered casserole that will cook while you're having fun doing something outdoors.

Spray a 4-5 quart crock pot with non-stick cooking spray. Completely cover the bottom of the pot with slightly crushed tortilla chips.

Brown ground beef in a skillet; drain fat, then add the ranch-style beans and their liquid and mix together. Combine soups, tomatoes, chili powder and onion in a separate bowl and blend well.

Layer half of the beef mixture over the chips, then half the soup mixture over the beef, ending with half the cheese over the beef. Repeat these layers once more beginning with chips and ending with cheese.

Cook on HIGH in crock pot for 2 ½ to 3 hours.

"If you reject the food, ignore the customs, fear the religion, and avoid the people, you might better stay home."

— James Michener

Crock Pot Enchiladas
Bonnie Keller, Blanchard, Oklahoma

6-8 Servings

- 1-2 pounds ground beef
- 1 cup chopped onions
- 1 (10 ½-oz.) can cream of chicken soup
- 1 (10 ½-oz.) can cream of mushroom soup
- 1 can chopped green chilies
- 1 (10 ½-oz.) can enchilada sauce
- 2 (10 ½-oz.) cans cheddar cheese soup
- 12 soft corn tortillas

Garnish:
- Salsa of your choice

Brown and drain the ground beef. Mix all ingredients together in a crock pot. Cook on LOW 8-10 hours (stir occasionally). One hour before serving, stir in tortillas that have been torn into pieces.

Bonnie says, "I keep a crock pot in the trailer. This dish will cook while I am fishing or hiking. When we get home, dinner is served." Her recipe resembles Chris' Crock Pot Mexican Fiesta, but uses a few different ingredients. Try them both! Serve topped with your favorite salsa.

"In Mexico we have a word for sushi: bait."
— José Simons

Casseroles and One-Dish Meals

Tamale Beef Slow-Cook

Linda Stewart, Burleson, Texas

6 Servings

- 1 pound ground beef (round)
- 2 cups chopped sweet onions
- 1 cup chopped bell pepper
- 2 (10 ½-oz.) cans mild tomatoes and green chilies
- 3 cups cooked pinto beans
- 1 (14-oz.) can cream-style corn
- 1 (10 ½-oz.) can beef broth
- 8 frozen beef tamales, thawed

Garnish:

Shredded cheddar cheese, optional

Linda's version of a Mexican-inspired casserole includes chopped beef tamales.

Brown meat with onions and peppers in a large pan until meat is cooked. Add tomatoes, corn, beans and broth and bring to a boil. Reduce heat and simmer. Chop tamales in small 1-inch pieces, add and heat through. Spoon into bowls and sprinkle with cheese if you like.

"Let your food be your medicine, and your medicine be your food."

— *Hippocrates*

Casseroles and One-Dish Meals

Green Chile Enchilada Casserole

Nicolas M. Lucero, On the road in Arizona

Serves a Crowd

- 4 cups diced cooked chicken
- 2 cups shredded jack cheese
- 3 (10-oz.) cans cream of mushroom soup
- 1 cup diced green onions
- 2 cups diced roasted mild green chilies, canned or fresh
- 1 cup water or chicken stock
- 3 dozen corn tortillas

Nicolas shared this recipe from his wife, Lucy. It fills two 9 1/2 x 11-inch baking dishes and is a real crowd-pleaser!

Place chicken, cheese, soup, green onions and chilies in a large bowl and mix. Add water or chicken stock.

Fry tortillas in hot oil and drain on paper towels.

In each casserole dish, place a layer of filling, then a layer of tortillas and continue layers, ending with filling. Bake at 375 F for 25 minutes.

Tip
Too Hot to Handle!
National Center for Home Food Preservation

Wear plastic or rubber gloves, and don't touch your face while handling or cutting hot peppers. If you don't wear gloves, wash hands thoroughly with soap and water before touching your face or eyes.

Casseroles and One-Dish Meals

Low-Carb Turkey Fajita Wrap

Nyla Diegel-Monville, Otisville, Michigan

4 Servings

- ½ cup olive oil, cold-pressed
- ½ red onion, chopped
- 2 sweet red peppers, chopped
- 1 clove garlic, minced
- 1 tablespoon ground cumin
- 1 teaspoon chili powder
- ⅛ teaspoon cayenne pepper
- 1 tablespoon fresh cilantro, chopped
- 1 fresh turkey breast, thinly sliced into strips
- Salt and pepper, to taste
- Red lettuce leaves

Serve up these lettuce wraps for a healthy, delicious and filling meal.

Add all ingredients to pan and sauté. Wrap mixture in red lettuce leaves with shredded monterey jack cheese, a sprinkle of cilantro and a dab of sour cream, if you like. Roll up lettuce and use toothpicks to secure.

"I've been on a constant diet for the last two decades. I've lost a total of 789 pounds. By all accounts, I should be hanging from a charm bracelet."

— Erma Bombeck

Casseroles and One-Dish Meals

Bud's Chicken and Dumplings

Clark "Bud" Lindsay, Hillsboro, Oregon

2 Serving

- 1 (6-oz.) can chicken
- 2 (10 ¾-oz.) cans chicken vegetable soup
- 1 tube large biscuits (from grocery refrigerated section)

Dump the can of chicken and the soup into a fairly large pan with a lid. Cover and bring to a LOW boil.

Place the biscuits on the top of the mixture and cook for 10 minutes with the lid off. Then replace lid and cook for another 10 minutes. Don't let it boil too hard or the dumplings will tear apart.

Here is an easy, quick and tasty dinner.

Says Bud: "Wrap up left over biscuits until you are ready to use them. Then heat a small fry pan on the old stovetop on LOW heat, cook until lightly browned, turn them over and when brown on both sides, you will have a nice hot biscuit."

Cast-Iron Cooking

Even though it's heavy, nothing beats cast iron cookware for versatility. It goes from stovetop to oven and is great on the grill.

Once seasoned, it needs little oil, because foods don't stick. Clean by just wiping or use some water (or even sand and water), but no soap. The best way to prevent rusting is to dry it on a hot grill or burner. When it gets really cruddy on the outside, heat on the grill until it's really hot and the burnt stuff will flake off.

Then re-season by heating slowly with a little oil, wipe clean, and it's as good as ever. Bargain-priced frying pans, dutch ovens and griddles can often be picked up at garage sales and thrift stores.

Casseroles and One-Dish Meals

Unstuffy Cabbage

Tony Troskoski, Rock Hill, South Carolina

4 Servings

- 1 **pound ground beef (chuck)**
- ¼ **teaspoon pepper**
- 1 **teaspoon salt**
- ½ **teaspoon minced garlic**
- ½ **onion, chopped fine**
- ¼ **cup uncooked rice**
- 1 **egg**
- 1 **(14-oz.) can sauerkraut**
- 1 **(10 ½-oz.) can tomato soup**
- 1 **tomato soup can filled with water**

Mix together raw beef, pepper, salt, garlic, onion, rice and egg. Form into ice-cream-scoop-sized meatballs and fry them in electric frying pan in 1 tablespoon cooking oil, browning all sides.

Drain grease from fry pan.

Drain kraut and rinse thoroughly. Lay the rinsed kraut on the bottom of frying pan and place fried meatballs on top. Mix tomato soup and water together, and then pour over the meatballs and kraut. Simmer for 1 hour. (Or cook 4 hours on LOW in crock pot.)

Tony says, "If you like Polish stuffed cabbage rolls, this meal tastes exactly the same, but without the work. The kraut does not add a sour taste, because it is rinsed first. Serve with mashed potatoes and corn.

"Your family will love this dish, and it will become one of your featured quick dishes on the road as well as at home." He adds, "If your dog sleeps in your bed, do not share this meal with him."

"Life expectancy would grow by leaps and bounds if green vegetables smelled as good as bacon."

— Doug Larson

Casseroles and One-Dish Meals

Skillet Spaghetti

Jon Leiendecker, Ohio City, Ohio

4 Servings

- 1 pound ground beef
- ¼ teaspoon pepper
- 2 tablespoons dried onion
- 1 teaspoon salt
- ¼ teaspoon garlic powder
- ½ teaspoon dry mustard
- 4 oz. spaghetti or linguini noodles, uncooked
- 1 (8-oz.) can tomato sauce
- 1 (3-oz.) can mushrooms, undrained
- 3 ½-4 cups tomato juice

Garnish:
- Parmesan cheese

Jon likes to make this dish in an electric skillet and says it works great. You don't have to cook the pasta separately.

Brown ground beef and drain fat. Sprinkle seasonings and dried onion over beef. Arrange spaghetti over the top. Pour the tomato sauce, mushrooms (and liquid) and juice over the spaghetti. Cover tightly and cook over LOW heat, stirring occasionally, for 15-20 minutes or until spaghetti is done.

To double, simply increase spaghetti to 8 oz. and use entire large can of tomato juice.

Casseroles and One-Dish Meals

Basic Impossible Pie and Variations

Pamela Burns, Burlington, Kentucky

4-8 Servings

Base (regular size):

- 1½ cups milk
- ¾ cup biscuit mix
- 3 eggs
- Salt and pepper, to taste

Base (large-size):

- 2 cups milk
- 1 cup biscuit mix
- 4 eggs
- Salt and pepper, to taste

Fillings (approximate):

- ½ to 1 cup chopped cooked meat
- ¾ to 1 cup shredded cheese
- ¾ to 1 cup chopped cooked or raw vegetables

Equipment:

Use a 9-inch pie pan or square baking pan for the regular size, or a large round or rectangular 9x13x2-inch baking dish for the large recipe.

Using a prepared baking mix, you can make a "pie" that forms its own crust as it bakes.

Heat oven to 400 F. Grease pie plate. Sprinkle filling ingredients (meat and/or vegetables and cheese) into pie plate. Beat base ingredients until smooth, 15-30 seconds in a blender, or 1 minute on high with a hand beater, or 2 minutes by hand. Pour into dish over filling. Bake approx. 25-35 minutes, until knife inserted in center comes out clean and top is golden brown. Cool 5 minutes before slicing to serve.

NOTES: Use any raw or leftover cooked vegetables, chopped into uniform-sized pieces (cook carrots and potatoes in the microwave first). Slice or chop raw veggies smaller than cooked. Thawed frozen spinach (squeezed dry) and frozen chopped broccoli work well.

Use any cooked or canned meat in uniform pieces.

Try all-veggie or all-cheese pies.

Add herbs/spices as desired.

Add mustard, horseradish, hot sauce or barbeque sauce to base if it seems appropriate, in small amounts.

Basic Impossible Pie Variations

Continued from previous page.

- **Chopped chicken, broccoli, jack cheese and chopped onion**
- **Chopped ham, mushrooms and Swiss cheese**
- **Bacon (6 slices, cooked, drained and chopped), broccoli and cheddar**
- **Tuna (one 6 ½-oz. can drained), tomato slices and cheddar**
- **Shrimp, leek and zucchini with smoked gouda**
- **Crumbled (cooked) hamburger, cheddar, green chiles (The Burger Pie)**
- **Spinach, gorgonzola and chopped walnuts**
- **Canadian bacon or diced pork with peas, mozzarella or smoked provolone**
- **Turkey, peas, green onion and dried cranberries (Thanks Again Pie)**
- **Three cheeses with asparagus (2 cups cheese)**
- **Sliced (cooked) potato, sliced onions and herb-flavored cream cheese**
- **Pork or chicken, green chilies and cheddar (pour red chili sauce over servings)**
- **Corned beef, diced (cooked) potatoes, hot sauce and Swiss**
- **Corned beef, rinsed and drained sauerkraut and Swiss (The Reuben)**
- **Bulk sausage (cooked), salsa and whole green chilies stuffed with cubes of cheddar or jack cheese (Rellenos Casserole)**
- **Roast beef, onion, green or red peppers and any cheese (The Philly)**
- **Chicken, chopped celery, onion, cashews and jack cheese**
- **Spinach, feta cheese, black olives and diced tomato (The Greek).**

Casseroles and One-Dish Meals

Skillet Chops with Beans
Jerry Ledyard, Salado, Texas

4 Servings

- 4 pork chops
- 1 (14-oz.) can pork and beans
- Brown sugar

Brown chops and set aside. To the same skillet, add a can of your favorite pork and beans. Warm the beans, then cover the top of the beans with the pork chops. Sprinkle brown sugar on top and simmer, covered, until pork chops are tender.

Jerry's recipe is quick and easy to fix after a day outdoors. Cole slaw would be a nice side dish, and corn bread, if you're feeling ambitious.

Sausage Jambalaya
Linda Prioux, Lumberton, Texas

4 Servings

- 1 pound link sausage (any kind), cut up
- 2 cups raw rice
- 1 large onion, chopped
- 1 large bell pepper, chopped
- 2 stalks celery, chopped
- ¼ pound butter or margarine, melted
- 1 (10-oz.) can chicken broth

Season to taste, depending on how spicy your sausage is. Put all of the ingredients into a rice cooker and stir to mix. Cook according to rice cooker directions, stirring occasionally.

Linda says this Cajun-style dish is easy to fix with any kind of sausage you prefer. Serve with a salad.

Casseroles and One-Dish Meals

Jimmy's Sausage Jambalaya

David Louviere, Ama, Louisiana

3-5 Servings

- 1 pound regular bulk sausage
- 1 pound hot bulk sausage
- 1 pound hot dogs, sliced
- 1 pound Polish sausage, sliced and cubed
- Garlic powder and Cajun seasoning, to taste
- 2 cups converted rice
- 1 (10-oz) can beef broth
- 1 (10-oz.) can French onion soup
- 1 broth can water
- 1 (16-oz.) can tomato sauce

Crumble and brown sausage with hot dogs and Polish sausage. Scoop out excess fat, leaving some for flavoring. Season to taste.

Put meats, rice, broth, soup, water and tomato sauce into large pot with cover. Cover and cook in 350 F oven for 1 hour. Stir and add water if rice needs to cook longer or is too dry. If necessary, cook additional 20 to 30 minutes.

David suggests adding other meats such as beef, shrimp or chicken.

Casseroles and One-Dish Meals

All-In-One Casserole

Phyllis and Miles Greer, Many, Louisiana

4 Servings

- 1 cup uncooked rice
- 4-6 chicken tenderloins or boneless chicken breasts (cut up if you wish)

Seasonings, to taste:
- Creole blend
- Onion powder
- Garlic powder
- Salt and pepper

- 1 (10 3/4-oz.) can cream of chicken soup
- 1 (10 ¾-oz.) can cream of mushroom soup
- 1 (10-oz.) can tomatoes with green chilies

Garnish:
- Shredded cheddar cheese

Here's a creamy chicken and rice casserole made on the stovetop.

Cook the rice. Season and lightly brown the chicken in a large skillet.

In a bowl, mix together the soups and tomatoes; pour into the skillet with the chicken and stir together. Cook a few minutes till the chicken is done. Sprinkle the top with the cheese, turn off the heat, put a lid on it and let it sit for a few minutes.

Casseroles and One-Dish Meals

Crawfish Pie

Julie Savoy, St. Amant, Louisiana

4-6 Servings

- 1 (¼ pound) stick butter
- 1 medium onion, chopped
- 1 medium bell pepper, chopped
- 2 ribs celery, chopped
- ½ cup green onion, chopped
- 1 (10 ½-oz.) can golden mushroom soup
- 1 (small) can evaporated milk
- 1 tablespoon cornstarch
- ½ teaspoon crab boil, or to taste
- ½ teaspoon salt, or to taste
- 1 tablespoon Creole seasoning, or to taste
- 2 9-inch pie crusts, ready-made
- 1 pound crawfish tails, whole

Using a heavy skillet, sauté onion, bell pepper and celery in butter until tender. Add soup, milk and cornstarch. Cook on MEDIUM heat for about 15 minutes.

Add green onions; lower fire to a simmer and cook for about another 20-25 minutes.

Using 9-inch pie plate, lay one piecrust on bottom of plate; fill with crawfish mixture; put remaining crust on top. Make a few vent holes by slicing top crust.

Bake at 350 F until pie has browned evenly, about 25 minutes. Let pie cool slightly before cutting.

"The most remarkable thing about my mother is that for thirty years she served the family nothing but leftovers. The original meal has never been found."

— Calvin Trillin

Casseroles and One-Dish Meals

Quick and Healthy Poached Haddock

Charlie Wallace, Buxton, Maine

4-6 Servings

4	shallots
2	cloves garlic, finely chopped or minced
½	pound mushrooms, sliced
	Kosher salt and pepper, to taste
	Extra-light olive oil
1	(14 to 15-oz.) can diced tomatoes
1	cup white wine
½	cup low sodium, no-fat chicken broth
2-3	pounds haddock

Heat a large skillet over MEDIUM heat. Add extra-light olive oil to coat the bottom of the skillet. Add the shallots and garlic and sauté until translucent, about 5 minutes. Add mushrooms and salt and pepper to taste. Add chicken broth and white wine, bring to a simmer and reduce to half the amount.

Turn heat to MEDIUM-LOW, add haddock, salt and pepper to taste (again), and diced tomatoes (over the haddock). Cook about 10-15 minutes and serve.

Delicious, easy, inexpensive and heart-healthy! Even the kids will eat this — "Mine do!" says Charlie.

"Why does Sea World have a seafood restaurant?? I'm halfway through my fish burger and I realize, Oh my God... I could be eating a slow learner."

— Lyndon B. Johnson,
former president of the U.S.

Casseroles and One-Dish Meals

Overnight Tuna Casserole
Elena Engelsman, Anaheim, California

2-4 Servings

1	(10 ¾-oz.) can cream of mushroom soup
1	cup milk
1	(6 ½-oz.) can water-pack tuna, drained and flaked
1	cup uncooked elbow macaroni
1	cup frozen green peas
½	cup chopped onion
1	cup shredded cheddar cheese

Whisk soup and milk in a 2-quart microwave-safe bowl until well blended. Stir in remaining ingredients. Cover and refrigerate overnight.

Cover with lid. Microwave on HIGH for 11 minutes or until bubbly.

Plan Ahead #2
Anita Leathers, East Lansing, Michigan

When at home, I fix huge servings of roast beef, meatloaf, lasagna, turkey, pork loin, etc. We eat one meal of each and then I divide up all the remainder into amounts my hubby and I can eat for a meal and put them into vacuum-type food-saver bags and label. When we head out, I have enough for 30 to 40 meals. On the road, I combine them with microwaved baked potatoes and either a salad or a quick veggie (canned or frozen) and we have a good meal without having to cook or shop. Anything that doesn't fit in my RV freezer stays at home in the deep freeze for the next trip. I also fry several pounds of hamburger meat and place it in ½-pound packages to use in casseroles for other quick meals. The whole point of camping and being on the road is to relax, not spend your whole time cooking or finding someplace to eat out!

Casseroles and One-Dish Meals

Cheesy Eggplant Parmesan

Betsy Monsalve, Erie, Pennsylvania

4 Servings

- 1 medium eggplant (about 1 pound)
- 1 egg
- 2 tablespoons milk
- 1 cup Italian-seasoned breadcrumbs
- 1 ¾ cups spaghetti sauce
- 2 cups part-skim mozzarella cheese, shredded
- 2 tablespoons freshly grated parmesan cheese

The microwave eliminates having to fry the eggplant, which is the traditional method of making this vegetarian dish. It is rich in calcium.

Peel the eggplant and cut it into ¼-inch thick slices. In a shallow bowl, beat the egg with the milk. Spread the breadcrumbs in a shallow plate. Dip the eggplant slices into the egg mixture, then into crumbs to coat well.

Arrange half of the eggplant in a 10-inch microwaveable plate lined with paper towels. Microwave, uncovered, on HIGH for about 4 minutes or until tender, rearranging the slices once halfway through the cooking time. Repeat with remaining eggplant.

Spread ¼ cup of the spaghetti sauce in an 8-inch square microwaveable baking dish. Layer half of the eggplant, half of the mozzarella cheese and half of the remaining spaghetti sauce in the dish; repeat layers. Sprinkle with the parmesan cheese.

Microwave, covered, on HIGH for about 4 minutes or just until hot. If you do not have a turntable in your microwave, rotate the dish; microwave on MEDIUM (50%) covered, for 10 minutes or until hot and bubbling, rotating the dish once halfway through the cooking time.

Let stand covered for 5 minutes, then serve.

Casseroles and One-Dish Meals

Broccoli Lasagna Bianca

Laurie Schollman, St. Louis, Missouri

8 Servings

- 1 (15- to 16-oz.) container fat-free ricotta cheese
- 1 cup egg substitute
- 1 tablespoon minced basil (or 1 teaspoon dried basil leaves)
- ½ cup chopped onion
- 1 clove garlic, minced
- 2 tablespoons margarine
- ¼ cup all-purpose flour
- 2 cups fat-free (skim) milk
- 2 (10-oz.) packages frozen chopped broccoli, thawed and well drained
- 1 cup (4 oz.) shredded part-skim mozzarella cheese
- 9 lasagna noodles, cooked and drained
- 1 small tomato, chopped (optional)
- 2 tablespoons grated parmesan cheese

Garnish:
Fresh rosemary or basil leaves

In medium bowl, combine ricotta cheese, egg substitute and minced basil; set aside. In large saucepan over MEDIUM heat, sauté onion and garlic in margarine until tender-crisp. Stir in flour; cook for 1 minute. Gradually stir in milk; cook, stirring until mixture thickens and begins to boil. Remove from heat; stir in broccoli and mozzarella cheese.

In lightly greased 13x9x2-inch baking dish, place 3 lasagna noodles; top with ⅓ each ricotta and broccoli mixtures. Repeat layers 2 more times. Top with tomato (if desired); sprinkle with parmesan cheese. Bake at 350 F for 1 hour or until set. Let stand 10 minutes before serving. Garnish with rosemary or basil leaves.

This low-fat, eggless lasagna is made with a creamy sauce flavored with basil and rosemary. Add a salad and crusty bread for a complete meal.

Casseroles and One-Dish Meals

Potato-Pepper-Spinach Frittata

Cheryl Dillon, Reno, Nevada

6 Servings

- 3 tablespoons olive oil
- 10 oz. baby Yukon gold potatoes, quartered
- 10 oz. peppers, any combination of sweet or hot
- 1 large sweet onion, cubed
- 1 teaspoons minced garlic
- 1 bunch spinach, rinsed, trimmed and chopped
- 6 large eggs
- Salt and freshly ground black pepper, to taste
- 4 oz. jack cheese, grated

Heat the oil in a large oven-proof or cast-iron skillet over MEDIUM-HIGH heat. Add the potatoes, and sauté until they begin to brown, about 10 minutes.

Add the peppers, onion and garlic, and sauté for about 7 minutes more, or until the peppers wilt and the onion softens. Add the spinach, reduce the heat to MEDIUM-LOW, and cover the skillet. Cook for about 3 minutes, or until the spinach wilts.

Beat the eggs well, seasoning with salt and pepper. Stir in shredded cheese.

Preheat the broiler. Uncover the skillet and stir potato mixture. Pour in the eggs, increase the heat to MEDIUM-HIGH, tilt the pan and lift the mixture to allow uncooked eggs to run underneath. Stir and continue cooking for about 5 minutes more.

Broil the frittata for about 1 minute, or until the top browns. Serve at once.

To accent this hearty vegetarian supper, brunch or lunch dish, season it with plenty of freshly ground black pepper. To provide the heat, select an assortment of peppers ranging from mild to hot. A California chardonnay would be a good wine for this dish — not too overpowering for the potatoes, peppers and spinach.

Casseroles and One-Dish Meals

Salads!

Summer Salad, page 67

Orzo Chicken Salad

Barbara Pearce, Jackson, Mississippi

4 Generous Servings

- 1 (16-oz.) package orzo, cooked and drained but not rinsed
- 1 pound boneless, skinless chicken thighs
- 1 teaspoon salt
- 1 teaspoon garlic powder
- 1 teaspoon pepper
- Olive-oil cooking spray
- 3 tablespoons olive oil, divided
- ½ cup chopped walnuts
- 2 teaspoons minced garlic
- 1 ½ cups sliced fresh mushrooms
- 12 medium green onions, chopped
- 1 sweet red pepper, chopped
- 1 yellow pepper, chopped
- 2 cups diced roma tomatoes
- ½ cup sliced black olives
- ½ cup shredded basil
- Mixed salad greens

Garnishes:
- Tomato wedges
- Basil leaves

Orzo is a small rice-shaped pasta that has a nice texture. Barbara made the finals in the 2003 National Chicken Cooking Contest with this recipe.

Sprinkle chicken with salt, garlic powder and pepper. Coat large fry pan with olive-oil cooking spray. Over MEDIUM-HIGH heat, cook chicken about 8 minutes on each side or until fork-tender and golden brown. Remove chicken and set aside.

In same pan, place 1 tablespoon olive oil over MEDIUM-HIGH heat; add walnuts, cook until golden brown; remove.

In same pan, place remaining 2 tablespoons olive oil; add garlic and mushrooms. Cook until mushrooms begin to change color; remove and set aside. Cut chicken into bite-size pieces and add orzo, mushrooms, onions, peppers, tomatoes, olives and basil.

Continued on next page ...

Orzo Chicken Salad
Continued from previous page ...

Lemon-Greek Dressing:

- ½ cup olive oil
- 4 tablespoons mayonnaise
- 3 tablespoons fresh lemon juice
- 3 tablespoons Greek seasoning

Lemon Greek Dressing: In medium bowl, mix together ½ cup olive oil, mayonnaise, lemon juice and Greek seasoning. Whisk until smooth.

Toss chicken mixture with dressing. Arrange mixed greens on serving plate. Top with chicken mixture, garnish with tomato wedges, basil leaves and reserved walnuts.

"The best things in life aren't things."
— Ann Landers

Make Salad Dressings Right in the Bowl!

A simple way to make fresh dressing for each bowl of salad is to mix the dressing right in the salad bowl and then add the greens.

If the salad will sit for a while before being served, try putting a shallow bowl or lid over the dressing before adding the greens; remove the bowl before tossing the salad. That way the greens do not get soggy sitting in the pool of dressing.

Salads

Chinese Chicken Salad

Margaret Shirley, Clearlake, California

12 Servings

- ½ cup vegetable oil
- ⅛ cup sesame oil
- 2 teaspoons salt
- ½ cup rice vinegar
- Pepper, to taste
- 2 packages ramen noodles, broken up (do not use the flavor packet)
- ¼ cup butter or margarine
- ⅓ cup sesame seeds
- ⅔ cup (4 oz.) slivered almonds
- 3 boneless, skinless chicken breasts, poached, cooled and cut into bite-sized pieces
- 1 medium head of green cabbage, finely chopped or shredded
- 1 bunch green onions sliced fine

Dressing: Combine oils, salt, rice vinegar and pepper to taste. (Best if mixed together several hours before serving.)

Sauté noodles, butter, sesame seeds and almonds until just golden brown. Combine all ingredients just before serving.

Margaret says this goes over really well at potluck dinners and can be made with shrimp if you like.

"Always remember that you are absolutely unique. Just like everyone else."

— *Margaret Mead*

Salads

Curried Chicken Salad

Mary Hurlburt, Cincinnati, Ohio

8 Servings

- 1 ½ cups cooked rice (white, wild or combination)
- 2 tablespoons salad oil
- 1 tablespoon rice vinegar
- 1 teaspoon salt
- ¾ teaspoon curry powder
- 2 cups cubed cooked chicken
- 1 cup chopped celery
- ¼ cup chopped green pepper
- 1 (10-oz.) package frozen peas, cooked
- ¾ cup mayonnaise
- Romaine or iceberg lettuce, shredded, or mixed salad greens in bag

Garnish:
- Prepared chutney (optional)

Another great potluck dish, with the exotic flavor of curry.

Combine rice, salad oil, vinegar, salt and curry powder. Combine chicken, celery, green pepper, peas and mayonnaise. Chill separately several hours or overnight. Mix together. Serve on greens and garnish with chutney.

"To remember a successful salad is generally to remember a successful dinner; at all events, the perfect dinner necessarily includes the perfect salad."

— *George Ellwanger*

Salads

Tomato-Garbanzo Pasta Salad with Salami

Colleen Hjelle, Agoura Hills, California

4-8 Servings

- 1 (6-oz.) jar marinated artichoke hearts, sliced lengthwise (reserve marinade)
- ¼ cup red wine vinegar
- 2 tablespoons chopped fresh basil or 1 ½ teaspoons dried
- 2 teaspoons finely chopped garlic
- 1 teaspoon salt
- ¼ teaspoon red pepper flakes
- Olive oil
- 12 oz. corkscrew, small shells or other pasta, cooked and drained
- 3 large tomatoes, seeded, diced and drained, or equivalent cherry tomatoes, quartered
- 1 (15 ½-oz.) can garbanzo beans, rinsed and drained
- 1 cup finely chopped green onions
- ½ cup sliced, chopped or salad olives, black or green
- ¼ pound salami or pepperoni sausage, sliced and cut bite-size (optional)
- ¼ cup finely chopped flat-leaf parsley

This will make at least 8 servings as a side dish or 4 as a main course. It's a great outdoor or picnic dish because it doesn't contain mayonnaise and needn't be refrigerated.

Combine vinegar and next four ingredients. Combine artichoke marinade and enough oil to make ½ cup; beat into vinegar mixture. Gently combine dressing with pasta, artichokes and remaining ingredients. Serve at room temperature.

Salads

Grilled Asparagus and Mushroom Salad

California Asparagus Commission

6 Servings

1	pound fresh asparagus, trimmed
	Olive oil, as needed
	Salt, as needed
	Freshly ground pepper, as needed
2	tablespoons fresh lemon juice
1	clove garlic, finely chopped
⅛	teaspoon crushed red pepper, or to taste
2	tablespoons olive oil
½	pound medium crimini or white mushrooms, cleaned
1 ½	oz. parmesan cheese, shaved paper thin (use a cheese planer or vegetable peeler)

Blanch asparagus: In a frying pan large enough to hold spears in one layer, bring approximately 3 inches of water to a boil. Stir in 1 tablespoon salt. Add asparagus. Cook at a medium boil until slightly underdone, about 3 minutes depending on thickness. Drain on paper towel and cool.

To grill, brush asparagus with olive oil. Grill asparagus over MEDIUM-HIGH heat, turning frequently, until lightly browned and fork-tender, about 5 minutes. Lightly season with salt and pepper. Cool. Cut at an angle in 1 ½-inch pieces, reserve.

To make vinaigrette, mix lemon juice, garlic, red pepper and ⅛ teaspoon salt; whisk in oil. Reserve. (Recipe can be made ahead to this point. Refrigerate cooled asparagus and vinaigrette, tightly sealed, if serving more than 2 hours later. Return to room temperature before continuing.)

Slice mushrooms about ¼-inch thick. Toss mushrooms with reserved asparagus and vinaigrette; arrange on a platter. Scatter shavings of parmesan over salad.

Grilling adds a smoky dimension to fresh asparagus, which pairs perfectly with mushrooms and cheese. Serve this as a salad or side dish.

Salads

California Summer Fruit Salad
California Fresh Apricot Council

5 Servings

- 2 cups sliced fresh apricots
- 1 ½ cups sliced fresh strawberries
- 1 ½ cups sliced fresh kiwi fruit
- ⅓ cup thinly sliced green onion
- 1 tablespoon finely chopped jalapeño peppers
- 1 tablespoon shredded fresh mint
- 1 tablespoon fresh lemon juice
- ½ teaspoon salt

Garnish:

Mint leaves

In a large bowl gently toss all ingredients. Arrange fruit on individual serving plates or a platter, or thread on wooden skewers for fresh-fruit kabobs.

Nutritious food makes us feel better. Try this recipe for good health and good eating. Apricots, strawberries and kiwi fruit combine to create a salad that bursts with color and flavor — perfect for late-spring and early-summer holidays and celebrations.

Salads

Summer Salad
Paula Nuotio, Kingsburg, California

4 Servings

- 4 tomatoes, cut into wedges
- 1 medium red onion, thinly sliced and separated into rings
- 1 burpless cucumber, sliced
- Zesty Italian dressing

Sometimes the simplest salads are the most refreshing, especially when tomatoes are in season. Heirloom tomatoes are especially interesting for this colorful salad. This recipe can be sized up or down depending on how many servings you need.

Place all ingredients in a bowl, toss with dressing about 1 hour before serving.

Variations: This basic salad can be embellished with feta cheese and kalamata olives for a Greek salad, or fresh mozzarella and basil for an Italian dish.

"It's okay to play with your food."
— Emeril Lagasse

Salads

Do-It-Yourself Salad Dressings — Inexpensive, Fast and Delicious!

Instead of packing prepared salad dressing, concoct your own using olive oil, vinegar, dijon mustard, salt and pepper. Add spices, minced onion, shallots and/or garlic, grated ginger, lemon juice, a dash of hot sauce or worcestershire sauce, catsup, juice or wine to taste.

General proportions are four parts oil to one part vinegar, but this can be varied as far as 1:1. The vinegar may be replaced by any citrus juice, or use a combination.

Add spices and salt to the vinegar and mix before adding the oil. Mix the dressing in a jar with a tight-fitting lid and store in the refrigerator for up to one week; bring to room temperature and shake before serving.

"Happiness is having a large, loving, caring, close-knit family in another city."

— *George Burns*

Pomegranate Jewel Spinach Salad
Pomegranate Council

6 Servings

- ½ teaspoon finely chopped lemon zest
- 2 tablespoons fresh lemon juice
- 2 teaspoons finely chopped shallot
- ¼ teaspoon ground cumin
- ¼ teaspoon salt
- 3 tablespoons olive oil
- 6 strips thick bacon, cut crosswise in ¼-inch pieces
- 8 oz. (about 9 cups, lightly packed) baby spinach leaves
- Seeds from 1 medium pomegranate, about ¾ cup
- 1 cup julienned daikon radish

Pomegranate seeds add garnet color, sweet-tart flavor and crispy crunch to this tasty salad. Bacon and daikon radish are savory counterpoints to the fresh ingredients.

To prepare dressing, whisk together lemon zest, juice, shallot, cumin and salt; whisk in oil. Reserve. Starting in a cold frying pan, cook bacon over MEDIUM heat, stirring occasionally, until almost crisp, about 5 minutes.

Drain on paper towel and cool. To assemble salad, toss spinach, bacon, pomegranate seeds and daikon with reserved dressing.

Salads

Cornbread Salad

Jim and Vicki Cooper, Depoe Bay, Oregon

4-6 Servings

- 1 small box cornbread mix, baked and cooled
- ¼ cup chopped or diced green pepper
- 2-3 large tomatoes, chopped
- 1 cup mayonnaise

Here's an unusual salad that should surprise your guests. Variations include adding any combination of the following: diced celery, onions, pickles, pimentos, drained canned beans or corn, diced green chilies, shredded cheese, hard-boiled eggs or crumbled crisp-cooked bacon.

Crumble the cornbread into a salad bowl and add green pepper and tomatoes. Add mayonnaise to consistency you prefer and let set 4-6 hours or overnight.

"To make a good salad is to be a brilliant diplomatist — the problem is entirely the same in both cases. To know how much oil one must mix with one's vinegar."

— *Oscar Wilde*

Soups & Stews!

Soups, Stews and Chili

White Navy Bean Soup

Rita Tate LeDoux, Broussard, Louisiana

3 Servings

- ¾ cup fully cooked ham, chopped
- 2 (14 ½-oz.) cans navy beans (or other beans of your choice)
- ½ bean can water
- 1 (4-oz.) can chopped mild green chilies (hot if you prefer)

Brown the ham in a dutch oven or kettle. Add beans, water and chilies. Simmer for about 15 minutes to heat through. Serve with crackers.

Just a few ingredients make this satisfying soup.

Quick 'n' Tasty Veggie Soup

Evelyn Allen, Dyer, Indiana

4 Servings

- 1 (14-oz.) can chicken broth
- 1 (14 ½-oz.) can diced tomatoes
- 1 (1-pound) package frozen mixed vegetables
- Salt, pepper and seasonings, to taste

Mix all ingredients together in a pot; bring to a boil; add salt, pepper or other seasoning if desired.

There are so many different frozen vegetable combinations available that this soup can have many ethnic variations — Southwestern, Mediterranean, Asian or all-American, using any spices you like. Use low-fat chicken broth to make a healthier soup.

Soups and Stews

Greek Egg and Lemon Soup

Kim Souza, Oak Park, California

4-6 Servings

- 1 (46-oz.) can of chicken broth
- 4 teaspoons or cubes of chicken bouillon
- ½ cup rice
- 3 eggs
- 1 ½ cups fresh lemon juice

Garnishes:
- Lemon slices
- Parsley

In a large saucepan combine the broth, bouillon and rice. Cover and cook on LOW heat until the rice is tender, about 20 minutes.

In a large bowl, beat the eggs well. Beat in the lemon juice. Slowly beat in about ⅓ of the hot chicken broth. Return all the broth to the saucepan. Continue to heat on LOW until the mixture becomes creamy and hot, stirring occasionally. Do not overcook or boil because the soup will curdle. If desired, garnish with lemon slices or parsley.

The Greeks have a word for it: *avgolemono*. **Great served with a warm, crusty bread.**

Soup Too Salty? All is Not Lost!

If your soup or stew is too salty, add a peeled potato or two, depending on how salty it is and how much you have in the pot. As the potato cooks, it will absorb a lot of the salt. The cooked potato can then be discarded, or used if you prefer.

If it is only a little salty, a little sugar or honey can be added to counteract it.

Soups and Stews

Classic Onion Soup

National Onion Association

6 Servings

- 4 large yellow onions, sliced
- 6 tablespoons butter or margarine
- 1 tablespoon sugar
- 2 quarts reduced-sodium chicken broth
- ½ cup brandy (optional)
- Salt and pepper, to taste
- ½ French-bread baguette, sliced, toasted
- Grated romano cheese

Melt butter in large saucepan that holds at least 4 quarts. Add onions; cook over MEDIUM heat, stirring often, 12 minutes or until tender and golden. Add sugar and cook, stirring, for 1 minute. Add broth; cover and bring to a boil.

Reduce heat; simmer 12 minutes. If desired, add brandy; cook 2 minutes. Season with salt and pepper.

To serve, ladle soup into bowl; float toast on soup. Sprinkle with cheese.

"Only the pure of heart can make a good soup."

— *Ludwig von Beethoven*

Soups and Stews

Tortellini Soup

Mary Southall, Healdsburg, California

4 Servings

- 1 (32-oz.) box of organic chicken stock
- 1 (9-oz.) package fresh tortellini
- 4-5 small zucchini, sliced thin
- Other leftover cooked vegetables, optional
- Pepper, to taste

Heat stock to boiling. Stir in tortellini and zucchini. Boil gently for 7-9 minutes and add pepper to taste.

Mary's secret is truly well flavored chicken stock. She says this soup is a great way to use up leftover vegetables and can be completely vegetarian if you choose meatless cheese tortellini.

Mom Lack's Salmon Chowder

Cynthia L. Bolick, Taylorsville, North Carolina

4 Servings

- 1 tablespoon butter
- 1 medium onion, chopped fine, sautéed, optional
- 1 (14-oz.) can salmon
- 6 cups milk
- Salt and pepper, to taste
- 1 (14 ½-oz.) can kernel corn, optional

If using onion, sauté in the butter and then add the other ingredients. Heat to just boiling.

Cynthia recommends serving the chowder garnished with cornbread crumbs, oyster crackers or saltines. It is especially good on chilly, damp days. It warms the heart, she says.

Soups and Stews

Quick Clam Chowder

Frances Froelich, Conroe, Texas

4 Servings

- 1 (6 ½-oz.) can minced clams with juice
- 1 (10 ½-oz.) can chicken gumbo soup
- 1 (10 ½-oz.) can pepper pot soup
- 1 (12-oz.) can evaporated milk

Mix together, heat just to the boiling point and serve.

Here's a quick recipe using pantry staples.

"As the days grow short, some faces grow long. But not mine. Every autumn, when the wind turns cold and darkness comes early, I am suddenly happy. It's time to start making soup again."

— Leslie Newman

California Avocado Tortilla Soup
California Avocado Commission

8 Servings

- **3 (14-oz.) cans chicken broth**
- **2 (10 ½-oz.) cans condensed tomato soup**
- **½ bunch cilantro, leaves only**
- **3 cloves garlic, finely chopped**
- **Cayenne, ground cumin and chili powder, to taste**
- **Diced grilled chicken breast, optional**
- **1 ripe avocado, seeded, peeled and cubed (reserve 8 cubes for garnish)**
- **8 corn tortilla chips, crumbled**

In a large pan combine chicken broth, soup, cilantro, garlic and pepper. Bring to a boil, decrease heat and simmer for 10 minutes.

Cool slightly, and puree in batches in a blender (optional). Return to pan, add avocado cubes (and diced chicken breast, if desired) and heat through. Ladle into soup bowls and garnish with reserved avocado cubes and crumbled tortilla chips.

For a healthy soup, use fat-free, lower-sodium or less-salt chicken broth and low-sodium tomato soup.

Soups and Stews

Campers' Beef Stew
Tim Culey, Jonesboro, Arkansas

4-6 Servings

- 2 (24-oz.) cans beef stew
- 1 tube of refrigerated biscuits or crescent rolls
- No-stick vegetable oil spray
- Heavy-duty aluminum foil

Line a dutch oven with the foil. Empty the stew into the pot. Arrange the biscuits or rolls on top. Place the dutch oven in hot coals and place more coals on the lid. Bake for approximately 15-20 minutes until the topping is golden brown and the stew is hot.

Enjoy a one-pot meal! Spray foil with oil spray for easier serving and easy cleanup.

Beef and Vegetable Stew
Kitty Baker, Salado, Texas

2-4 Servings

- 1 (24-oz.) can beef stew
- 1 (14 ½-oz.) can stewed tomatoes (original, Mexican, Italian or any kind you choose)
- 1 (14 ½-oz.) can mixed vegetables, drained
- Other leftover or canned vegetables, optional
- Worcestershire sauce, to taste

This variation also uses canned beef stew, with added vegetables. Kitty says freshly baked cornbread tastes really good with this stew.

Heat together in a kettle and serve.

Tadhg's Irish Chili

Tim Culey, Jonesboro, Arkansas

8-10 Servings

- 2 pounds lean ground beef
- 2 large cans chili beans
- 2 medium cans chili con carne
- Canned tomatoes, to taste
- Chili powder, to taste
- ½ cup brown sugar
- 1 medium onion, sliced and diced, to garnish

Garnish:

- 1 (14 ½-oz.) can pitted, sliced ripe black olives

Brown and crumble ground beef in iron skillet and break up large pieces. Cover and keep hot while preparing rest of chili.

In a large crock or pot, mix chili beans, chili con carne and tomatoes and let simmer (LOW heat) for ½ hour or until bubbles begin to pop on surface. Stir quite often so nothing sticks or scorches on bottom.

Now sprinkle in the chili powder and brown sugar and mix thoroughly. Add the browned and crumbled ground beef. Mix thoroughly. Add the diced onion. Mix thoroughly. Now simmer (LOW heat) for 15 minutes.

Tim doesn't think the size of cans is very important — he says just to use whatever you have on hand or can find in the market. Chopped onions may also be sautéed with the ground beef or added with the vegetables. He serves this chili, with a garnish of raw onion and olives on top of each serving, accompanied by crackers, to his hungry friends. Any leftovers can be frozen. "Tadhg" is Timothy in Gaelic.

"To be one, to be united is a great thing. But to respect the right to be different is maybe even greater."

— Bono

Soups and Stews

Mike's Firehouse Chili
Michael Poole, Seattle, Washington

16 Servings

- 1 pound bacon, diced
- 2 medium onions, chopped
- 6 cloves garlic, peeled and crushed
- 2 jalapeño peppers, seeded and diced
- 2 red chili peppers, seeded and diced
- 1 habanero pepper, seeded and diced
- 3 pounds beef chuck, cut in 1-inch cubes
- 4-5 Louisiana spiced sausage links
- 1 (28-oz.) can crushed tomatoes
- 1 (28-oz.) can diced tomatoes
- 1 (6-oz.) can tomato paste
- 8-10 tablespoons chili powder
- 2 tablespoons cumin seeds
- 1 tablespoon oregano
- 1 tablespoon thyme
- 2 tablespoons sugar
- 3 cups beef stock, divided
- 3 (15-oz.) cans pinto beans
- 1 can or "smart pack" chili with beans
- 2 tablespoons masa (corn flour)
- 1 tablespoon crushed red pepper

Cayenne pepper, salt and ground black pepper, to taste

Garnishes:

Chopped green onions

Grated cheddar cheese

Sour cream

Fresh chopped cilantro for

Firefighter Michael Poole of the Seattle Fire Alarm Center took top honors in the National Five-Alarm Hormel Chili Cook-Off with his oh-so-hot chili.

In a large saucepan or dutch oven over MEDIUM heat, fry bacon until fat is rendered and bacon is crisp. Drain off all but 2 tablespoons of the bacon fat into another large skillet. Add onions, garlic and peppers to the first pot and cook until soft, 10-15 minutes. Meanwhile, in the large skillet over MEDIUM-HIGH heat, brown the

Continued on next page ...

Soups and Stews

Mike's Firehouse Chili

Continued from previous page ...

Treat the peppers with respect; use rubber gloves or wash your hands thoroughly after dicing them!

chuck and sausage in the reserved bacon fat (or vegetable oil). Add the browned meat to the vegetables in the pot.

Use 1 cup of the stock to deglaze the browning pan. Add that stock, the tomatoes, tomato paste, seasonings, the other 2 cups stock, pinto beans and chili to the large pot. Bring to a simmer. Add masa and crushed red pepper.

Reduce heat, cover and simmer over LOW heat about 1 hour or until meat is tender. Season to taste with dashes of cayenne pepper, salt and pepper. Serve with garnishes on the side.

"Next to jazz music, there is nothing that lifts the spirit and strengthens the soul more than a good bowl of chili."

— *Harry James*

Soups and Stews

Chili
with Zucchini, Sausage and Beans
Bill Davey, Rogersville, Alabama

4 Servings

- 2 tablespoons olive oil
- 1 green pepper, cut into bite-size pieces
- 1 medium onion, cut into bite-size pieces
- 2 pounds hot Italian sausage, casings removed
- 4 medium zucchini, cut into bite-size pieces
- Salt and pepper, to taste
- 1 (12-oz.) jar salsa, mild, medium or hot
- 2 (14 ½-oz.) cans kidney beans
- 2 tablespoons tomato paste
- Cinnamon and allspice, to taste

In a dutch oven or other large kettle, heat olive oil and sauté onion and green pepper. Add sausage and cook until it is no longer pink inside.

Add a layer of zucchini, salt and pepper. Cover and cook about 10 minutes. Add salsa, beans and tomato paste and pinches of cinnamon and allspice. Stir and heat through.

Bill's chili sounds like just the thing for a coolish evening!

"Wish I had time for just one more bowl of chili."

— *Last words of Kit Carson*

Outdoor Cooking!

Beef Sirloin Kabobs, page 91

Miner's Packet

Spencer McDaniel, "The California Gold Miner," Wilseyville, California

Serves a Crowd

10-pound beef tri-tip roast

Heavy-duty aluminum foil

Mixed vegetables of your choice

Chili powder, to taste

Garlic powder, to taste

Bottled salsa

Spencer says this beef tri-tip is even better the next morning, made into awesome burritos with jumbo tortillas and eggs — if there's any left over!

This recipe requires a deep bed of hot coals, so start the fire in plenty of time.

Place the roast, vegetables and seasonings on the foil, then fold the foil over everything and seal the edges airtight.

Using a shovel, create a crater in the center of the campfire coals and placed the wrapped roast in the crater. Cover the top of the package with hot coals.

Stretch more aluminum foil over the entire campfire and cover that with dirt or sand, leaving a small "breathing hole" in two corners.

Let cook for 4-6 hours, uncover the package, dust it off and dig in.

Is my steak done yet?

Rare meat should feel like the area between your thumb and index finger when your hand is relaxed — soft and spongy — when you press it with the index finger of your other hand. Medium-rare is how that same area feels when you form a loose fist. Medium is how that same area feels when your fist is tightly clenched — firm, with a little give. We won't even mention well-done steak.

Outdoor Cooking — BEEF

Todd's Best Steak
Charles Cawood, Houston, Texas

1 Serving

- 1 steak of your choice for each person
- Seasoned salt
- Teriyaki sauce

This is a recipe that Charles' son Todd came up with after many trials. The sugar in the teriyaki sauce seals in the juices and gives the steaks classic grill marks. Charles says these are the best steaks he's ever eaten.

Let steaks warm at room temperature for 20 minutes while grill is heating (on HIGH heat setting). Sprinkle seasoned salt liberally on both sides, then sprinkle teriyaki sauce on both sides.

Place steaks on hot grill and turn once after 1 ½ to 3 minutes. Use a digital meat thermometer to check doneness. If additional cooking is needed, turn the heat down, as the steaks will finish cooking quickly.

"A bath and a tenderloin steak. Those are the high points of a man's life."

— Curtis Siodmak

Outdoor Cooking — BEEF

Asian Grill Mammoth Ribs

Cattlemen's Beef Association

6 Servings

- 5 pounds beef back ribs
- ¼ cup finely chopped jalapeño peppers
- 2 tablespoons minced fresh ginger
- ½ cup catsup
- ⅓ cup Dijon-style mustard
- ⅓ cup hoisin sauce
- 2 tablespoons water
- 2 tablespoons packed brown sugar

Garnish:

Chopped fresh cilantro

These huge ribs look prehistoric! Sprinkle with chopped cilantro and serve with Asian greens, rice pilaf and vegetables.

In small bowl, place jalapeño, ginger, catsup, mustard, hoisin sauce and water; whisk until blended. Reserve ½ cup marinade for basting and add brown sugar to it.

Place ribs in large resealable plastic bag; add marinade and turn to coat. Close bag securely; marinate ribs in refrigerator 1 to 4 hours, turning occasionally. Remove ribs from marinade and discard the used marinade.

Prepare charcoal grill for INDIRECT cooking by igniting an equal number of charcoal briquets on each side of fire grate, leaving open space in the center. When coals are MEDIUM, ash-covered (25 to 30 minutes), add 3 to 4 new briquets to each side. Position cooking grid with handles over coals so additional briquets may be added when necessary.

Place ribs, meat side up, in large (16x11x2-inch) foil roasting pan; cover tightly with aluminum foil. Place foil pan on cooking grid; cover with grill lid and grill over MEDIUM heat 1 to 1½ hours or until ribs are fork-tender.

Carefully remove roasting pan from grill; remove ribs from pan and place, meat side up, on grill rack. Baste ribs with reserved marinade and grill, covered, 10 to 15 minutes, turning and basting occasionally.

Maui-Wowie BBQ Beef Ribs

Lynn R. Frary, Seattle, Washington

6 Servings

- **1 cup of soy-garlic marinade** (You can substitute ginger garlic sauce or apricot marinade)
- **¼ cup water**
- **¼ cup low-salt soy sauce**
- **2-4 tablespoons fresh ginger, chopped fine**
- **3 cloves garlic, crushed**
- **½ (16-oz.) can crushed pineapple** (or just pour in the whole can)
- **2 tablespoons warm honey** (or 2 tablespoons brown sugar or 2 packets of artificial sweetener)
- **Wasabi paste or pepper sauce to suite your crowd's tastes**
- **2 tablespoons extra-virgin olive oil**
- **Pepper, to taste**
- **3-4 pounds of beef cross-cut (flank style) ribs, bone in.** Ask your butcher to cut them this way for you.

Mix sauce ingredients well and add to ribs in a resealable plastic bag. Refrigerate for at least two hours. Can be made up ahead of time — marinate overnight or even freeze for later use!

Barbecue over MEDIUM heat to heat the bones through without overcooking the meat. Brush on leftover marinade while cooking.

Serve with fresh papaya, pineapple and gingered white rice — you'll have a taste of Hawaii!

Foil-roasted Barbecued Beef Ribs

Lee A. Yager, Omaha, Nebraska

I wrap my beef ribs, covered in sauce (1 part bottled sauce with additional honey and onions) in two layers of aluminum foil. I put them on the grill for 1½ hours at 350 F, then open up the package and paint them with more sauce and finish cooking them on an open grill. The meat always falls off the bone.

Outdoor Cooking — BEEF

Beefsteak and Potato Kabobs
Cattlemen's Beef Association

4 Servings

- 1 pound all-purpose potatoes, cut into 1 ½-inch pieces
- ¾ cup steak sauce
- 2 large cloves garlic, minced
- 1 pound boneless beef top sirloin steak, cut 1 inch thick and into 1 ¼-inch-square pieces
- 1 medium yellow or zucchini squash, cut into 1 ¼-inch chunks

Double-pronged metal skewers are handy for kabobs; the food is secured and can't spin while cooking. You can add other vegetables, such as mushrooms, tomatoes or peppers, to this recipe; firm ones should be microwaved first (see at right for potatoes), so everything cooks evenly.

Place potato pieces in microwave-safe dish; cover with vented plastic wrap. Microwave on HIGH 6 to 8 minutes or until just tender, stirring once. Cool slightly.

Combine steak sauce and garlic in 1 cup glass measure. Microwave on HIGH 1 ½ minutes, stirring once.

Cut squash lengthwise in half, then into 1 ¼-inch pieces. Cut beefsteak into 1 ¼-inch pieces. Combine beef, squash, potatoes and ⅓ cup sauce in large bowl; toss. Alternately thread beef and vegetables onto metal skewers.

Place kabobs on grid over MEDIUM, ash-covered coals. Grill, uncovered, about 10 to 12 minutes for medium-rare to medium doneness, turning occasionally and brushing with remaining sauce during last 5 minutes.

Outdoor Cooking — BEEF

Campfire Stew

Donna Gazo, Greenville, North Carolina

6 Servings

- 1 pound hot dogs, sliced ½-inch thick, or 1 pound ground beef, browned
- **Onions, sautéed, optional**
- 1 (10 ½-oz.) can bean and bacon soup
- 1 (14 ½-oz.) can kernel corn
- 1 (14 ½-oz.) can lima beans
- 1 (14 ½-oz.) can boiled potatoes, cut into small dice
- 1 (14 ½-oz.) can green beans
- **Other leftovers or canned vegetables, optional**
- **Salt, pepper, and other seasonings, to taste**

Donna says this stew should be made a day ahead so the flavors meld.

Mix and bring to a boil over the campfire or on the stove, season to taste and simmer.

Americans eat an average of 60 pounds of beef yearly.

— *U.S. Department of Agriculture*

Outdoor Cooking — BEEF

Southwestern Popper Beef Burgers

Iowa Beef Industry Council

4 Servings

1	pound ground beef
¼	cup prepared thick-and-chunky salsa
4	frozen cream-cheese or cheddar-stuffed jalapeño peppers
¼	cup prepared salsa con queso
¼	cup chopped plum tomatoes
2	tablespoons sliced pitted ripe olives
4	English muffins, split, or hamburger buns

Combine ground beef and chunky salsa in large bowl, mixing lightly but thoroughly. Lightly shape into four thin patties. Place one stuffed pepper in center of each patty; wrap beef around pepper to enclose, sealing seams and forming ball. Flatten balls into patties. Patties will be about 4 to 5 inches across and 1 inch thick.

Place patties on grill over MEDIUM-HOT, ash-covered coals. Grill, uncovered, 15 to 16 minutes for MEDIUM (160 F) doneness, turning occasionally, until beef is not pink in center and juices show no pink color.

Spread 1 tablespoon salsa con queso evenly over top of each burger. Sprinkle evenly with tomatoes and olives. Serve on muffins.

What's a camping trip without burgers? Try these, with a surprise inside, for a change of pace.

Outdoor Cooking — BEEF

Beef Sirloin Kabobs
with Roasted Red Pepper Sauce
Cattlemen's Beef Association

6 Servings

- 1 tablespoon olive oil
- 1 medium onion, finely chopped
- 3 cloves garlic, minced
- 2 (7-oz.) jars roasted red peppers, rinsed, drained, finely chopped
- 1 cup dry white wine
- 2 tablespoons tomato paste
- ¾ teaspoon dried thyme leaves, crushed, or 2 teaspoons minced fresh thyme
- 1 cup beef broth
- 1 teaspoon cornstarch
- 1 ½ pounds boneless beef top sirloin steak, cut 1 inch thick
- 2 teaspoons coarse ground black pepper
- ¾ teaspoon salt
- ¾ teaspoon sweet paprika
- 2 cloves garlic, minced

Dipping Sauce: Heat oil in large skillet over MEDIUM heat until hot. Add onion and 3 cloves garlic; cook and stir 2 to 3 minutes or until onion is tender. Add red peppers, wine, tomato paste and thyme, stirring until tomato paste is blended.

Combine broth and cornstarch in small bowl, mixing until smooth. Stir into pepper mixture; bring to a boil. Reduce heat to MEDIUM-LOW; simmer 10 to 12 minutes or until slightly thickened, stirring occasionally. Keep warm.

Meanwhile cut beefsteak into 1¼ x 1¼ x 1-inch pieces. Combine pepper, salt, paprika and 2 cloves garlic in large bowl. Add beef; toss to coat. Thread beef pieces evenly onto six 12-inch metal skewers, leaving small space between pieces.

Place kabobs on grid over MEDIUM, ash-covered coals. Grill, covered, about 7 to 9 minutes for medium-rare to medium doneness, turning once. Serve with dipping sauce.

No steak knives are needed for these bite-size steak dippers.

Outdoor Cooking — BEEF

Grilled Rosemary Garlic Tenderloin

Chloetta Welch, Fairfield, California

4 Servings

- 2 tablespoons fresh rosemary (3 large sprigs)
- 3 large garlic cloves
- 2 full tablespoons honey
- 1 tablespoon Dijon mustard
- ¼ cup balsamic vinegar
- 2 tablespoon rice vinegar
- ½ cup extra-virgin olive oil
- 1 pound pork tenderloin

Chop the rosemary until minced. Place the garlic cloves in a food processor or blender along with rosemary until finely minced. Add the honey, mustard, vinegars and olive oil. Process until smooth. Reserve 1 cup for sauce.

Place tenderloin in a resealable plastic bag and add remaining marinade. Seal and refrigerate for at least 4 hours or overnight.

Preheat the grill to 375 F. Drain the marinade and place pork on the grill. Cook until internal temperature registers 150 F; usually takes about 30 minutes. Turn often to avoid burning. Slice thin and serve with the remaining marinade.

Chloetta likes to serve this aromatic pork with wild rice.

Outdoor Cooking — PORK

Grilled Pork Tenderloin with Tomatillo and Onion Salsa

National Pork Board

4 Servings

1	pork tenderloin, about 1 pound
1	tablespoon olive oil
1	teaspoon ground cumin
	Dash salt and ground black pepper
10	medium green tomatillos, outer skin removed
2	small jalapeño peppers
1	large onion, cut into ½-inch thick slices
3	tablespoons water
½	cup chopped fresh cilantro, plus additional for garnish

Tomatillos have a slightly tart flavor and are a good source of Vitamin C.

Butterfly pork tenderloin lengthwise. Flatten pork with the palm of your hand to achieve even thickness. Cover with oil and season with cumin, salt and pepper.

Prepare grill for MEDIUM-HIGH heat. Grill tomatillos, jalapeños and onion for about 5 to 10 minutes, turning often, until soft. Remove vegetables from grill. Seed and stem jalapeños. Put tomatillos, tomatoes, jalapeños and half the onions into a blender or food processor; blend until mixture becomes a thick paste. Transfer to a serving dish and mix in water and cilantro, adding salt to taste.

Place pork on the grill and cook for 3 to 4 minutes on each side, or until internal temperature as measured with an instant-read thermometer is 160 F. Slice pork and arrange on a warm serving tray. Spoon some of the tomatillo mixture and remaining grilled onions over the pork. Garnish with cilantro. Serve with remaining sauce.

Outdoor Cooking — PORK

Smokin' Succulent Grilled Pork Chops

Don D. Lusby, Shediac, New Brunswick

8 Servings

- 1 cup mayonnaise
- 2 tablespoons lime juice
- 2 tablespoons chopped cilantro
- 2 cloves garlic, finely chopped
- 1 teaspoon chipotle chili pepper
- 8 pork chops

Don makes his sauce ahead of time and keeps it in the refrigerator for up to two days.

In a medium bowl, combine all ingredients except chops. Reserve ½ cup mayonnaise mixture to serve with chops.

Grill chops, turning once and brushing frequently with mayonnaise mixture until chops are done. Serve with reserved mayonnaise sauce mixture.

Pork ranks third in annual U.S. meat consumption, behind beef and chicken, averaging 51 pounds per person.

— U.S. Department of Agriculture

Outdoor Cooking — PORK

Peachy Baked Dutch-Oven Pork Chops

Bob Lunceford, Clarksville, Tennessee

6 Servings

- 6 pork chops (center cut with bone)
- Salt and pepper, to taste
- 1 box stuffing mix for pork
- 4 tablespoons butter, melted
- 1 ¼ cups hot water
- 1 (15-oz.) can sliced peaches
- ¼ cup apricot preserves
- 1 tablespoon Dijon mustard
- 1 tablespoon dry minced onion

Start your charcoal fire ahead of time so the coals will be ready for use.

In a 12-inch dutch oven, combine stuffing mix (including seasoning packet), butter, hot water and juice from peaches: stir to mix and then spread evenly. Season pork chops with salt and pepper, arrange over of stuffing.

In a small bowl, mix together preserves, mustard and minced onion. Spoon preserve mixture over chops. Put sliced peaches over the top. Cover dutch oven and bake, using 8-10 briquettes on bottom and 16-18 on top of dutch oven for 60 minutes.

Sweet baby back ribs?
Don Frye, San Diego, California

Try par-boiling using cola (make sure it doesn't boil over onto your stove). Then barbecue the ribs and, just before they are done, brush your favorite barbecue sauce on each side. Guaranteed, they will be the tastiest ribs you ever barbecued.

Outdoor Cooking — PORK

2-Mees Baby Back Ribs
Pete Toomey, Matthews, North Carolina

4 Servings

- 1 slab baby back ribs
- Garlic salt
- Freshly ground black pepper
- Louisiana rub
- Prepared barbecue sauce of your choice

Lay ribs on board or platter and sprinkle with garlic salt, pepper and Louisiana rub, but do not rub it into the meat. Wait 30 minutes, turn the ribs over and repeat. Cover and refrigerate for at least 2 hours.

Preheat the grill and add ribs, meaty side down, to the LOW-HEAT area of the grill for INDIRECT cooking. Cook about 1 hour and turn with tongs. Cook another 45-50 minutes and check the temperature with an instant-read thermometer; it should reach 170 F. Let the ribs sit for 2 to 3 minutes. Brush with sauce — don't over-sauce — and let the ribs rest for another minute or so to soak. Cut in 2-4 rib sections.

Pete swears these are some of the best ribs you will ever eat! Use tongs to turn the ribs, because a fork will puncture the meat and let the juices escape.

"Sex is good, but not as good as fresh, sweet corn."

— Garrison Keillor

Outdoor Cooking — PORK

Bayou Barbecued Ribs

Ron Sonnier, Breaux Bridge, Louisiana

2 Servings

- **2 pounds pork loin ribs**

Dry Spice Rub:
- 1 cup chili powder
- 1 tablespoon garlic granules
- 1 teaspoon onion powder
- ½ teaspoon cumin
- 1 ½ teaspoons salt
- 2 tablespoons seasoned salt

Sauce:
- 4 cups canned tomato sauce
- ½ cup diced tomato
- ¼ cup firmly packed brown sugar
- ¼ tablespoon Worcestershire sauce
- 2 tablespoons dried onion
- ¼ cup soy sauce
- ¼ cup water

Ron says you absolutely have to serve coleslaw and grilled corn on the cob as accompaniments. Prepare the dry spice rub at home before your trip and it'll be good to go.

Combine the dry ingredients for the spice rub in a jar. Rub ribs well with some of the mixture and refrigerate, covered, for 4 to 6 hours. (Store leftover spice rub in the covered jar for future use.)

In a saucepan, combine tomato sauce, tomato, sugar, Worcestershire sauce, onion, soy sauce, water, and ½ cup dry spice rub and cook over very LOW heat for 3 hours.

Preheat a grill or smoker over LOW heat until hot. Add ribs and cook, covered, for 3 to 5 hours. Brush with sauce during last minutes of cooking. Serve with remaining sauce.

"Never eat more than you can lift."

— *Miss Piggy*

Kansas City-Style Pork Back Ribs

Chef Paul Kirk, author of "Paul Kirk's Barbecue Sauces Cookbook"

4 Servings

- 3 slabs pork back ribs
- ½ cup sugar
- ¼ cup paprika
- 3 tablespoons seasoned salt
- 2 tablespoons chili powder
- 2 tablespoons ground black pepper
- 1 tablespoon celery salt
- 1 tablespoon onion powder
- 1 tablespoon garlic powder
- 2 teaspoons ground sage
- 1 teaspoon dry mustard
- 1 cup of your favorite barbecue sauce
- ½ cup honey

In pint jar with tight-fitting lid, combine sugar, paprika, seasoned salt, chili powder, black pepper, celery salt, onion powder, garlic powder, ground sage and dry mustard. Place lid on jar: shake jar to combine thoroughly. Set spice rub aside. Makes about 1 ½ cups.

In small saucepan over LOW heat, stir together barbecue sauce and honey. Heat through, stirring occasionally, about 5 minutes.

Set barbecue glaze aside, keep warm or at room temperature before using. (If storing for more than 2 hours, cover and refrigerate. Reheat gently before using.)

Pat ribs dry with paper towels and season generously with spice rub, using about 4-6 tablespoons for each slab of ribs.

Grill over INDIRECT heat in a covered grill or smoker for 1 ½ to 2 hours. Turn ribs once during cooking, about halfway through. Ribs are done when the meat is very tender (insert a paring knife between ribs to determine); they will pull apart fairly easily.

About 20 minutes before ribs are done, baste heavily with barbecue glaze. If you like your ribs extra sticky, baste again 10 minutes before removing from the grill.

North Carolina Pulled Pork BBQ Sandwiches

National Pork Board

10-12 Servings

- 2 cups cider vinegar
- ¼ cup packed brown sugar
- 1 tablespoon red pepper flakes
- 1 tablespoon worcestershire sauce
- 1 teaspoon salt
- Hot pepper sauce, to taste
- 1 5- to 5 ½-pound boneless pork shoulder roast
- Salt and pepper to taste
- 4 cups wood chips (use hickory or oak chips for the best flavor)
- 10 to 12 hamburger buns, split and toasted
- Coleslaw (optional)

Top with coleslaw for a crunchy, cool contrast. Have your favorite side dishes and some cold watermelon for dessert.

For gas grills, preheat and then turn off any burners directly below where the food will go. The heat circulates inside the grill, so turning the food is not necessary.

In medium bowl, combine vinegar, brown sugar, red pepper flakes, worcestershire sauce, salt and hot pepper sauce. Divide sauce into two portions and set aside.

At least 1 hour before grilling, soak wood chips in enough water to cover; drain before using. Rub meat with salt and black pepper. In a charcoal grill with a cover, place pre-heated coals around a drip pan for MEDIUM INDIRECT heat. Add ½-inch hot water to drip pan. Sprinkle half of the drained wood chips over the coals.

Place meat on grill rack over drip pan. Cover and grill about 4 hours or until meat is very tender. Add more preheated coals (use a hibachi or a metal chimney starter to preheat coals), wood chips and hot water every 1 to 1 ½ hours. Remove meat from grill; cover with foil and let stand for 20-30 minutes.

Using a fork, shred meat into long, thin strands. Pour sauce over shredded meat; toss to coat. Serve on toasted buns. If desired, top meat with coleslaw. Serve remaining sauce on the side.

Outdoor Cooking — PORK

Arkansas Slow-Smoked Ham *with Bourbon Sauce and Glazed Sweet Potato Packets*

National Pork Board and Reynolds Kitchen

16 Servings

1	6- to 7-pound cooked, bone-in ham
1	cup catsup
⅓	cup finely chopped onion
⅓	cup honey
⅓	cup cider vinegar
¼	cup bourbon
2	tablespoons prepared mustard
2	tablespoons lemon juice
1	teaspoon dried thyme, crushed
1	teaspoon minced garlic
½	teaspoon red pepper flakes
3	cups wood chips (use hickory or oak chips for the best flavor)

Sauce: In medium saucepan combine catsup, onion, honey, vinegar, bourbon, mustard, lemon juice, thyme, garlic and red pepper flakes. Bring to a boil. Reduce heat and simmer, uncovered, for 10-15 minutes or until desired consistency, stirring frequently. Divide sauce into two portions; set aside.

At least 1 hour before grilling, soak wood chips in enough water to cover; drain before using. In charcoal grill with cover, place preheated coals around a drip pan for MEDIUM-LOW INDIRECT heat. Sprinkle half of the wood chips over the coals.

Place ham on the grill rack over drip pan. Cover and grill for 2 to 2 ½ hours, until internal temperature (measured with a meat thermometer) is 140 F., basting with one portion of sauce the last 15 minutes. Remove ham from grill. Cover and let rest for 15 minutes before slicing. Reheat second portion of sauce and serve with ham.

Add more preheated coals (use a hibachi or a metal chimney starter to preheat coals) and wood chips halfway through grilling. Put sweet-potato packets on the grill after the ham has cooked for 2 hours.

Continued on next page ...

Glazed Sweet Potato Packets
Continued from previous page ...

4	sheets (18x24-inch) heavy-duty aluminum foil
8	large sweet potatoes, peeled, sliced
1 ⅓	cup orange marmalade
1	cup packed brown sugar
2	teaspoons ground cinnamon
4	tablespoons margarine, melted

Preheat grill to MEDIUM. Center 2 sweet potatoes on each sheet of foil; set aside. Combine orange marmalade, brown sugar, cinnamon and margarine; spread over sweet potatoes. Bring up foil sides. Double fold top and ends to seal, making four large foil packets, leaving room for heat circulation inside. Grill, covered, 20 to 25 minutes or until sweet potatoes are tender.

Easy-Does-It Ribs
John Ewing, La Verne, California

4 Servings

4	pounds spareribs
1	(10 ½-oz.) can tomato soup
2	tablespoons soy sauce
2	tablespoons honey
2	tablespoons minced onion
½	teaspoon Worcestershire sauce
¼	teaspoon minced ginger

Tomato soup is the main ingredient in John's sauce.

Precook the ribs in the oven or on a grill. Combine the soup with remaining ingredients in a saucepan and simmer for about 10 minutes.

Drain ribs and brush with sauce. Place ribs on a grill about 6 inches above coals and cook for about 30 minutes, turning and basting frequently.

Outdoor Cooking — PORK

Grilled Pizza *with Prosciutto, Parmesan and Asparagus*

Weber-Stephen Products Co.

1 (12-inch) Pizza

- 12 spears asparagus
- 3 tablespoons olive oil, divided
- ¼ cup cornmeal or all-purpose flour, for rolling dough
- 1 4-inch ball prepared dough, or purchased frozen dough, at room temperature
- 1 cup grated parmesan cheese
- 2 oz. prosciutto or Black Forest ham, finely sliced
- Sea salt and freshly ground pepper, to taste

Pizza on the grill is fun to make and fun to eat! This basic recipe can be varied with different combinations of cheese, vegetables and meat. Let everyone make their own.

Grill asparagus: Coat spears with 1 tablespoon olive oil, season with salt and grill 8 minutes over DIRECT heat, turning ¼ rotation every 2 minutes. Cut into 1inch pieces and set aside.

Lightly sprinkle a work surface with cornmeal or flour. Place dough directly in the middle of the work surface. Roll out gently into either a 12-inch rectangle or circle, ¼-inch thick. Brush both sides with olive oil and set aside until ready to grill.

Gently place dough in center of the cooking grate, directly over MEDIUM heat for 2-4 minutes, until the bottom of the crust is well marked and browned. Remove pizza from grill and sprinkle cheese generously over cooked side of crust.

Top with ham and asparagus, making sure to spread evenly over crust. If using a gas grill, switch to INDIRECT heat. Return pizza to the cooking grate and cook with lid closed until bottom is well browned, toppings are warm and cheese is bubbly, about 5-10 minutes. Remove from grill and season with pepper to taste. Slice and serve immediately.

Greek Lamburgers *with Cumin Yogurt in Pita Pockets*

Nelson and Sam Greaves, Waterford, Michigan

4 Servings

- ¼ teaspoon cumin seed
- ½ cup plain yogurt
- ⅛ teaspoon salt
- Pinch coarse ground black pepper
- 1 pound ground lamb
- 2 teaspoons mint, or 2 tablespoons fresh, chopped
- ⅓ cup feta cheese, crumbled
- 8 kalamata or black olives, pitted and finely chopped
- 4 pita breads, cut in half

Cumin Yogurt: Toast cumin seeds, in a preheated, dry skillet over MEDIUM heat, about 30 seconds or until aromatic. Remove from skillet. Crush in small bowl or with a mortar and pestle. Combine yogurt with the toasted cumin, salt and pepper. Set aside.

Combine lamb and next 3 ingredients in a mixing bowl. Gently form into 1-inch thick patties and season with salt and pepper to taste. Broil burgers 5 minutes per side or until lamb is done. Serve burgers in pita-bread pockets topped with cumin yogurt.

These Mediterranean-flavored burgers will make your friends say, "Opa!"

*"Red meat is not bad for you.
Now blue-green meat,
that's bad for you!"*

— *Tommy Smothers*

Buffalo Burgers on Focaccia
with *Pesto and Roasted Peppers*
Buffalo Groves, Inc.

3-4 Servings

- 1 pound ground buffalo meat
- Garlic salt and Worcestershire sauce, to taste
- 3-4 slices provolone cheese
- Focaccia bread
- Olive oil
- Prepared basil pesto
- Roasted red bell peppers, sliced

Form 3 or 4 burgers from the ground buffalo meat. Cook on the barbecue about 5 minutes on each side, sprinkling with the garlic salt and worcestershire sauce. When almost done, top with provolone cheese and let the cheese melt slightly.

Meanwhile, cut the bread, brush the cut sides with olive oil and lightly toast on the grill. Place the burgers on the bread and top with some pesto and a few slices of red bell pepper.

Don't squish the burgers when you flip them! You can use either fresh grilled red peppers or store-bought in a jar. Serve with your favorite salad or slaw.

Better Burgers!

Avoid pressing the ground meat when shaping hamburgers; use a light touch. To avoid a domed burger with dry edges, make about a ¼-inch depression in the middle of the burger and it will puff slightly when cooking to form an even surface. If you like your burgers well-done, make a hole in the center of the burger and it will cook evenly without drying out.

Outdoor Cooking — BUFFALO

R.C.'s Beer Butt Chicken

R.C. Kremer, Mountain View, California

4 Servings

- 1   3- to 6-pound chicken
- 1   6 pack (16-oz. cans) of your favorite canned beer (for marinating the chicken and the grill chef)
-     Lemon-pepper seasoning
- 4   cloves crushed garlic
- 1   lemon or orange (½ wedged and the rest sliced)

The beer moistens the chicken from the inside. It also keeps the chef from getting overheated.

Pour ½ can of beer into the cook and place the crushed garlic into the remainder of the can of beer and set aside, (1 hour minimum). The longer the beer sets, the better it will work (flat beer works best).

Go on ahead and have a full beer at this time, because you know that the half-can that you just had won't let you stop thinking about a full one.

Prepare an INDIRECT fire in your grill (300-350 F). Clean the chicken (won't need the giblets, save for fishing) and pat dry with paper towels. Spray the chicken with olive oil and season with lemon pepper inside and out. Make sure you get seasoning under the skin. You can even place lemon slices (or oranges) under the skin (held in place with toothpicks).

When the grill is ready, place the chicken over the ½ can of beer, and using the chicken's legs to form a tripod, place chicken on the center of the grill rack. Close the opening at the top of the chicken by stuffing the lemon or orange wedges into the opening.

The beer can should hold up the chicken, however there are inexpensive chicken racks on the market. Make sure that the chicken and beer are not directly over the flames and close the grill.

Continued on next page ...

Outdoor Cooking — CHICKEN

R.C.'s Beer Butt Chicken

Continued from previous page ...

Now would be a good time to crack another beer and pour it into the cook, while you reflect on what you just accomplished. Don't peek into the grill too many times (you know you want to).

Make sure that you use an instant-read thermometer to check the chicken (probe deep into the thigh, staying away from the bone). R.C. starts checking at 45 minutes and then at 10-minute intervals after that. Remove from the grill when 160 F at the thigh. Let stand 10 minutes and dig in.

Cooking times can vary (45 minutes to 2 hours) depending on the size of the bird and the grill temperature. The remainder of the beer should be poured into the cook throughout the grilling process (it may be shared, but R.C. doesn't recommend it, unless you start with a 12-pack, which he recommends for a larger bird).

Spicy Chicken Wings
Randie Lee Van Ness, Deltona, Florida

4 Servings

- 2 pounds chicken wings, thawed, whole or drumettes
- 1 package Louisiana crab boil (yellow cellophane package)
- 1 lemon, halved, if desired

Randie Lee's wings can also be served as an appetizer.

In a large pot boil enough water to cover wings. Add crab boil (watch your nose), lemon and wings. Bring back to boil, taking care not to let it boil over, for five minutes. Remove from heat and let stand for one hour and drain. (Can make ahead of time and refrigerate.) Then grill or broil until golden brown.

Mahogany Broiled Chicken with Smokey Lime Sweet Potatoes and Cilantro Chimichurri

Camilla Saulsbury, Bloomington, Indiana

4 Servings

- 1½ pounds boneless, skinless chicken breast halves, cut in 1-inch cubes
- 1 cup chopped cilantro leaves
- 6 tablespoons extra-virgin olive oil
- 3 large cloves garlic, minced
- ½ teaspoon salt, divided
- ¼ teaspoon pepper, divided
- 5 tablespoons dark brown sugar
- 3 tablespoons Dijon mustard
- 2 tablespoons bottled hoisin sauce
- 2 teaspoons balsamic vinegar
- ½ cup plus 1½ teaspoons lime juice, divided
- 2 large sweet potatoes, peeled, cut in ½ inch pieces
- 2 tablespoons unsalted butter
- 1 teaspoon chopped canned chipotle pepper
- 1 teaspoon adobo sauce (from canned chipotle)
- ¾ teaspoon ground cumin
- ½ teaspoon lime zest

Garnish:

- Cilantro sprigs

Camilla won first place at the 2005 National Chicken Cooking Contest with this recipe.

In small bowl, mix together chopped cilantro, olive oil, minced garlic, ¼ teaspoon of the salt and ⅛ teaspoon of the pepper; set aside.

In medium bowl, mix together brown sugar, mustard, hoisin sauce and vinegar. Reserve ⅔ of this mixture. To remainder, add ½ cup lime juice and stir in chicken; cover and refrigerate.

Place sweet potatoes in a heavy saucepan and cover with boiling water. Cook, covered, over medium high heat until tender, about

Continued on next page ...

Outdoor Cooking — CHICKEN

Mahogany Broiled Chicken

Continued from previous page …

15 minutes. Reserve ¼ cup cooking liquid, then drain potatoes in colander. Return potatoes to reserved cooking water and add butter, chipotle pepper, adobo sauce, remaining 1 ½ teaspoons lime juice, cumin, lime zest, remaining ¼ teaspoon salt and remaining ⅛ teaspoon pepper. Mash potatoes.

Thread chicken on 8 bamboo skewers that have been soaked in water. Grill or broil about 6 inches from heat, basting with reserved mahogany sauce until done, about 8 minutes.

To serve, divide potatoes among 4 plates; top each with 2 skewers of chicken and drizzle with cilantro chimichurri sauce. Garnish with cilantro sprigs.

Seafood Stuffed Chicken

Tracy Cole, Williamson, New York

4 Servings

- 2 whole chicken breasts
- 2 cups white cooking wine
- 1 (8-oz.) package frozen imitation crab or lobster
- ½ cup breadcrumbs
- Garlic, minced, to taste
- ¼ cup chopped spinach (frozen, thawed, squeezed dry)
- 1 (13-oz.) can artichoke hearts, cut into small chunks
- ½ cup mayonnaise or margarine
- Cheddar or parmesan cheese, optional
- Salt and pepper, to taste

Tracy says she loves to cook and "winged" this awesome recipe. She likes to serve it with wild rice and corn on the cob. Remember, cooking wine has added salt, so use less salt than usual when seasoning.

Butterfly the chicken breasts. Marinate for at least 2 hours in the wine.

In a large bowl, mix the cooked crab or lobster meat, breadcrumbs, garlic, spinach, artichoke hearts, mayonnaise or margarine. Stuff the filling in the chicken breast and fold to enclose. Sprinkle with salt, pepper and optional cheese and wrap tightly in oil-sprayed foil.

Grill in a cast-iron pan sprayed with cooking oil, not too close to the flame. If you are cooking in an oven, then you don't need to foil the chicken, but tie it with kitchen twine so it won't unroll.

"You can tell how long a couple has been married by whether they are on their first, second or third bottle of Tabasco."

— Bruce Bye

Outdoor Cooking — CHICKEN

Chicken Plantain Fajitas *with Mango Salsa*

Stephanie Howard, Oakland, California

4 Servings

3	boneless, skinless chicken breast halves
½	cup pineapple juice
1	tablespoon bottled jerk marinade seasoning
8	(10-inch) tortillas
4	tablespoons cooking oil, divided
2	ripe plantains, peeled, cut in half crosswise and cut in ½ inch slices
1	sweet red pepper, cut in strips
1	sweet yellow pepper, cut in strips
1	green bell pepper, cut in strips
8	green onions, cut in 1-inch strips
⅓	cup bottled sweet and sour sauce
1	tablespoon light rum

Stephanie's recipe took her to the National Chicken Contest finals.

Slice chicken across grain into thin strips; place in plastic bag set in shallow dish. In small bowl, mix together pineapple juice and jerk marinade seasoning; pour over chicken and marinate in refrigerator 30 minutes.

Wrap tortillas in foil and place in 350 F. oven about 10 minutes to heat through. Keep warm.

In large fry pan over MEDIUM heat, place 2 tablespoons of the oil. Add plantains and cook about 2 minutes or until golden brown; remove from pan. To pan, add pepper strips and onions; cook about 2 minutes until tender; remove from pan.

Drain chicken, add remaining 2 tablespoons oil to fry pan, add chicken and cook about 5 minutes. Return vegetables to pan; stir in sweet and sour sauce and rum. Add plantains and cook 1 more minute. Fill warm tortillas with chicken mixture. Arrange on platter and garnish with peppers, cilantro and lettuce. Serve with mango salsa.

Continued on next page ...

Chicken Plantain Fajitas
Continued from previous page ...

Mango Salsa:

1	large mango, peeled and finely diced
¼	cup diced red onion
¼	cup chopped cilantro
1	finely minced jalapeno pepper
¼	cup lime juice
½	teaspoon salt
¼	teaspoon pepper

Garnish:

2	each serrano (red), fresno (yellow), small jalapeno (green) and Thai chili (orange) peppers
	Cilantro leaves
	Red leaf lettuce

Mango Salsa: In medium bowl, mix together mango, red onion, cilantro, jalapeño pepper; lime juice, salt and pepper.

Give it a rest!

Baked, roasted or broiled meat should be allowed to rest after cooking. The juice will reabsorb into the meat, instead of ending up on your cutting board or plate.

Outdoor Cooking — CHICKEN

Pacific Rim Chicken Burgers with *Ginger Mayonnaise*

Kristine Snyder, Kihei, Hawaii

4 Servings

Chicken Burgers:

- 1 ¼ pounds ground chicken
- ⅔ cup panko (coating)
- 1 egg, lightly beaten
- 2 green onions, thinly sliced
- 3 tablespoons chopped cilantro
- 1 clove garlic, minced
- 1 teaspoon Asian hot chili sauce
- 1 teaspoon salt
- 1 tablespoon vegetable oil
- ½ cup bottled teriyaki glaze
- 4 teaspoons honey
- 4 sesame buns, split and toasted
- 4 leaves red lettuce
- 1 cucumber, peeled, seeded, halved and thinly sliced lengthwise
- Cilantro sprigs

Ginger Mayonnaise:

- ½ cup mayonnaise
- 2 teaspoons sweet pickle relish
- 2 teaspoons minced fresh ginger
- 2 teaspoons lime juice
- 1 clove garlic, minced
- ¼ teaspoon salt

Kristine was the National Chicken Cooking Contest first-prize winner, thanks to these burgers.

Ginger Mayonnaise: In small bowl, mix together mayonnaise, relish, ginger, lime juice, garlic and salt.

In large bowl, mix together chicken, panko, egg, onions, cilantro, garlic, chili sauce and salt. With oiled hands, form into 4 patties.

In small bowl, mix together teriyaki glaze and honey. Put oil in large nonstick fry pan over MEDIUM-HIGH heat. Add chicken and cook, turning and brushing with teriyaki glaze, about 10 minutes or until done.

Place burgers on toasted buns and top with lettuce, cucumber and Ginger Mayonnaise. Garnish with additional cilantro and cucumber slices.

Pulled-Turkey Barbeque

Bill O'Bier, Richmond, Virginia

8-10 Servings

- 1   5-7 pound turkey breast, thawed
- 2   bottles of your favorite barbecue sauce
-      Hot sauce to your taste

Toppings:
- Coleslaw
- Chopped onions

Roasted turkey breast replaces pork in this updated version of pulled pork.

Spray unheated grill rack and turkey breast with nonstick spray. Prepare grill for MEDIUM INDIRECT-heat cooking. Place roast on rack over drip pan. Cover grill and cook 1 to 1 ¼ hours or until meat thermometer in thickest part reads 170 F.

Let turkey stand 10 minutes before slicing. With your hands or two forks, pull all the turkey meat into shreds and place in a 4-quart crock pot or slow cooker. Add the barbecue sauce and hot sauce and mix well. Place cooker on LOW setting and heat 2 to 3 hours until all the flavors have blended.

Easy-Good Barbecue Sauce

Tim Culey of Jonesboro, Arkansas, starts with store-bought sauce and then jazzes it up to make 2 ½ cups.

- 1   (16-oz) jar of your favorite brand of barbecue sauce
- 1 ½   cup brown sugar
- 1   large onion, chopped fine
- 3   large bell peppers, chopped fine
- 3-4   capfuls Italian salad dressing
- ¼   cup catsup
- 4   shakes Worcestershire sauce
- 1   teaspoon prepared mustard

Mix all ingredients in saucepan or skillet. Simmer until onions and bell peppers are tender.

Outdoor Cooking — TURKEY

Goat Cheese-Stuffed Turkey Burgers with Roasted Red Pepper Relish

Linda Maikowski, Plano, Texas

6 Servings

Roasted Red Pepper Relish:

- 3 tablespoons olive oil
- 1 (7-oz.) jar roasted sweet red peppers, rinsed, drained, patted dry, chopped
- 1 ½ cups chopped onions
- 3 teaspoons finely chopped garlic
- 4 ½ tablespoons cider vinegar
- 3 tablespoons sugar (or sugar-free sweetener)
- ¼ teaspoon dry mustard
- ¼ teaspoon cayenne pepper

Roasted Red Pepper Relish: Heat oil in heavy large skillet over MEDIUM-HIGH heat. Add red peppers and sauté 2 minutes. Add onions and garlic. Cook until onions are tender, stirring frequently, about 5 minutes.

Mix vinegar and sugar in small bowl until sugar dissolves. Stir vinegar mixture into red peppers. Mix in mustard and cayenne pepper. Season with salt.

Continue cooking relish until all liquid has evaporated, stirring frequently, about 6 minutes. Cool to room temperature. (Can be prepared 1 day ahead. Cover and refrigerate. Bring to room temperature before using.) Makes about 2 cups.

Continued on next page ...

"I wish the bald eagle had not been chosen as the representative of our country... The turkey is a much more respectable bird, and withal a true original native of America."

— *Benjamin Franklin*

Outdoor Cooking — TURKEY

Goat Cheese-Stuffed Turkey Burgers

Continued from previous page ...

Goat Cheese-Stuffed Turkey Burgers:

- 1½ pounds lean ground turkey
- 6 tablespoons fresh breadcrumbs
- 3 tablespoons fresh lemon juice
- 2 teaspoons grated lemon peel, optional
- 2 teaspoons dried thyme
- 1⅛ teaspoon salt
- ½ teaspoons ground black pepper
- 6 tablespoons soft fresh goat cheese (such as Montrachet)
- 6 whole-wheat hamburger buns

The goat cheese and relish keep these burgers especially moist.

Combine turkey, breadcrumbs, lemon juice, lemon peel, thyme, salt and pepper in large bowl. Mix well. Divide turkey mixture into 6 equal portions. Form 1 portion into two 4-inch diameter patties. Place 1 tablespoon goat cheese atop 1 turkey patty; place second patty atop cheese. Seal patties at edges to enclose cheese.

Repeat with remaining 5 portions. (Can be prepared 4 hours ahead. Cover and refrigerate.)

Prepare barbecue (MEDIUM-HIGH heat). Grill burgers until cooked through, about 5 minutes per side. Grill hamburger buns, cut side down, until lightly toasted, about 1 minute. Place turkey burgers on bottom half of buns. Top burgers with Roasted Red Pepper Relish, then bun tops.

Skin Deep ...

Dry rubs with spices add a lot of flavor to grilled meats. Salt is a must and can be combined with spices and seasonings; sugar can be added for a bit of caramel crunch. Coat the food surface entirely, but not too heavily; cover and refrigerate for 15 minutes to 2 hours or even overnight.

Deep-Fried Turkey

R.C. Kremer, Mountain View, California

Serves a Crowd

Turkey fryer with temperature gauge

1   12-15 pound turkey, thawed

    Dry rub of your choice

3-5 gallons peanut oil

Keep safety in mind. Make sure that you have the fryer positioned out of the wind on a level, non-flammable surface.

Cook in an area where you can control curious onlookers, especially children, pets and adults under the influence of intoxicants.

This fryer tips over very easily and a wind gust can cause it to tip. Never place a lid on the fryer when the burner is lit. Never leave the fryer unattended.

Have an all-purpose fire extinguisher on hand. Do not use water to put out a hot-oil fire!

If you just have to deep-fry your turkey, this is the best way to determine the amount of oil needed and to keep from burning anything up or down. (R.C. recommends no alcohol consumption during cooking.) Following these basic steps should make your deep-frying experience a success, even for a first-timer.

Keep in mind that turkeys are not all the same size. Do not measure using a frozen turkey; you will not get an accurate reading. Put the turkey in the empty fryer and add water to cover the turkey plus about one inch over. Remove the turkey and measure the water.

An easy way to measure is to use a tape measure from the top of the pot to the top of the water and then measure the same distance on the outside of the pot and mark it. Remove the water and dry out the pot with paper towels.

Replace the water with the same amount of peanut oil. Set the turkey out on a counter covered with newspaper and foil for no more than an hour. (We cannot be too careful with poultry.) Dry the bird inside and out, using paper towels. Add a dry rub with your hands if you like.

Heat the oil to 380 F. (This is about 30 degrees above the recommended temperature

Continued on next page ...

Deep-Fried Turkey

Continued from previous page ...

of 350 F.) Be careful not to exceed this temperature because your oil might start to smoke and then start a fire. Wearing gloves, carefully and slowly lower the turkey into the hot oil — the slower the better. The temperature will drop 20-30 F after you place the turkey into the hot oil.

Because the oil was overheated, keep an extra eye on the temperature gauge; it will tend to rise. Do not let the temperature fall below 340 F. When adjusting the heat, do it gradually.

Deep-fry the turkey approximately 3 ½ minutes per pound at 350 F (i.e., 42 minutes for a 12-pounder and 52 minutes for a 15-pounder). Remove the turkey and let it set for 30 minutes before carving.

Trashcan Turkey

Rita LeDoux, Broussard, Louisiana

Serves a Crowd

- Metal trashcan with lid
- Heavy-duty foil
- Disposable aluminum roasting pan and V-rack
- 1   10-12 pound turkey
- ½   cup garlic, chopped, minced or mashed
- 1   cup butter, melted
- ¼   cup paprika or spices of your choice
- 2   cups of your favorite stuffing (optional)

Rita says the beauty of this is that once the turkey is positioned under the overturned trashcan, you don't have to do anything else — no bastin', no turnin', no nothin' — just wait.

And the cleanup is neat, too; just wrap up the foil and foil pan and toss them away. But not the trashcan — you're going to want to make this again.

Season the turkey with the garlic, butter and spices. Stuff if desired.

Place layers of heavy-duty foil on the ground in a 3-foot-square configuration. Place two bricks on the foil, a roasting pan on the bricks and a rack over the pan. Place the turkey on the rack, breast up. Invert the trashcan over the entire affair.

In the trashcan lid, light coals, using 1 pound of charcoal for every pound of turkey. When the coals are white, shovel them all around the bottom edge of the trashcan (actually the top rim) on the ground, reserving just enough coals to cover the top (actually the bottom) of the trashcan. Wrap the excess foil that is sticking out at the bottom around the coals.

Cook the turkey for 8 minutes per pound (for example, 80 minutes for a 10-pounder).

"I cook with wine, sometimes I even add it to the food."

— W. C. Fields

Outdoor Cooking — TURKEY

E-Z Salmon
Jim Willeford, Fort Worth, Texas

4-6 Servings

- 2 medium-size fresh salmon fillets
- ½ cup soy sauce
- ½ cup water
- 1 tablespoon freshly grated ginger
- 1 tablespoon dark brown sugar
- 4 cloves fresh garlic, minced
- Extra-virgin olive oil

Jim prefers to take the skin off the salmon for a less fishy taste, but he says it has to be handled more carefully to keep the meat from breaking up. He serves it with rice and a vegetable and says it's quick and easy with little cleanup.

Wash salmon and pat dry. Place in large resealable plastic bag. Mix soy, water, ginger, brown sugar and garlic in a bowl with a whisk and add to bag. Close the bag, let set for about 15 minutes and turn it over for another 15 minutes.

Oil fish and place over MEDIUM heat (DIRECT) grill and cook on each side for approximately 6-8 minutes or until fish flakes.

"Salmon are like men: too soft a life is not good for them."
— *James de Coquet*

Outdoor Cooking — FISH

Bob Lee's Caramelized Salmon *from the Great Northwest*

Bob Lee, founder of Country Coach Inc., Junction City, Oregon

16 Servings

1 (15-pound) fresh northwest coho salmon, filleted and de-boned, (leave the skin on), tail removed if you wish

Brown sugar

"This makes a mess out of the barbecue grill, but, boy, is it good!" says Bob.

Cover the salmon with as much brown sugar as you can pile on. Place on the HOT grill, but far enough from the heat so the skin doesn't burn.

After about 25 minutes, it should be caramelized. If not completely caramelized, cover with an aluminum foil tent for a few moments. Take the fish off the grill, leaving the skin on the grill.

Poached Salmon Filet *or Tuna Steaks*

Ken Seaver, Fort Worth, Texas

4 Servings

1 ¾ pound salmon fillet or 4 (¼-pound) tuna steaks

Extra-virgin olive oil

Garlic salt or your favorite seasoning blend

Ken suggests serving either fish with a nice white wine and swears it will melt in your mouth!

Lay out fillet or steaks on heavy aluminum foil, big enough to enclose the fish. Drizzle with olive oil and sprinkle seasoning over it. Wrap fish tightly in the foil and pinch the foil to seal contents.

Grill over a MEDIUM-HIGH gas or charcoal grill for 10-12 minutes. Unwrap and serve.

Smoke-Cooked Salmon Steaks with Pineapple Pecan Salsa

Susie Almazan, Thousand Oaks, California

6 Servings

- 1½ cups chopped fresh pineapple
- ½ cup chopped red onion
- ¼ cup packed cilantro leaves, finely chopped
- 1 jalapeño pepper, seeded and chopped
- ¼ teaspoon salt
- ¾ cup chopped pecans, toasted
- 6 fresh salmon steaks, 1-inch thick
- 2 or 3 lemons
- 6 tablespoons butter, melted
- 1 teaspoon curry powder OR ½ teaspoon crushed rosemary, (optional)
- ½ teaspoon salt
- ½ teaspoon freshly ground pepper

Here's a simple way to add a nice smoky flavor to the salmon.

About 30 minutes before serving, combine the pineapple, red onion, cilantro, jalapeño and salt to make salsa; set aside.

Make a drip pan out of heavy-duty foil large enough to hold all the steaks. Cover the base of the pan with thin slices of lemon and place the salmon steaks on top. Mix together the butter and curry powder or rosemary. Pour the mixture over the steaks and lightly season them with salt and pepper.

Arrange the charcoal to produce MEDIUM heat and place the pan with the steaks on the grill. Cover with the grill lid and occasionally add wood chips to produce smoke. Cook for about 45 minutes (basting occasionally with juices from the pan) or until the fish flakes easily with a fork.

The Chinook or King Salmon is the largest salmon in North America and can grow up to 126 pounds.

— Alaska Dept. of Fish and Game

Outdoor Cooking — FISH

Grilled Rainbow Trout Adobo with Roasted Corn Salsa

Wayne Oden, Hartford, Connecticut

4 Servings

- 1 cup dry white wine
- ½ cups fresh lime juice (remove zest before juicing to use for garnish)
- 1 tablespoons prepared adobo sauce
- 1 tablespoons finely chopped garlic
- 4 (8-oz.) rainbow trout fillets, butterflied
- Olive oil, as needed
- 4 cups field greens

Garnish:
- Lime zest and lemon zest as needed

Wayne's recipe won second prize in the Clear Springs Foods "Create a Classic" recipe contest.

Thoroughly mix wine and next 3 ingredients. Pour over fillets; let marinate 2 hours.

Remove fillets from marinade; pat dry. Heat ½ cup salsa in a little olive oil; keep warm. On a well-oiled grill, preferably fueled with wood, grill trout flesh-side down for 2 minutes. Turn; cook until just firm, about 1 minute. To serve, lay trout on a small bed of greens. Spoon warmed salsa over and beside trout. Garnish with lime and lemon zest.

Continued on next page …

Outdoor Cooking — FISH

Roasted Corn Salsa

Continued from previous page ...

- 1 cup roasted or grilled corn kernels
- ½ cup diced green chilies
- ½ cup diced plum tomatoes
- 2 tablespoons diced red onion
- ¼ cup fresh lemon juice (remove zest before juicing to use for garnish)
- 2 tablespoons chopped fresh cilantro
- 1 tablespoon prepared adobo sauce
- 1 tablespoon diced jalapeño pepper
- ¾ teaspoon coarse salt
- ½ teaspoon crushed red pepper flakes

Make Roasted Corn Salsa: Combine corn, chilies, tomatoes, red onion, lemon juice, cilantro, adobo sauce, jalapeño pepper, salt and red pepper flakes and let stand at least 20 minutes to marry flavors.

"In the hands of an able cook, fish can become an inexhaustible source of perpetual delight."

— *Jean-Anthelme Brillat-Savarin*

Grilled Stuffed Rocky Mountain Trout *with Fresh Corn Cakes*

Julie Frand, Van Nuys, California

4 Servings

- ¼ cup finely chopped red onion
- ¼ cup finely chopped green sweet pepper
- 2 teaspoons tarragon vinegar or white wine vinegar
- 1 teaspoon snipped fresh basil
- ¼ teaspoon salt
- ¼ teaspoon ground cumin
- ⅛ teaspoon pepper
- 1 tablespoon grated parmesan cheese
- 4 (8-10-oz.) fresh pan-dressed rainbow trout
- 2 tablespoons cooking oil

For stuffing: In a mixing bowl stir together the onion, sweet pepper, vinegar, basil, salt, cumin and pepper. Add parmesan cheese; mix well.

Rinse fish and pat dry with paper towels. Brush the outsides and cavities of fish with oil. Spoon one-fourth of the stuffing mixture into each fish cavity.

Brush a wire grill basket with cooking oil. Place fish in basket. Grill fish on an uncovered grill directly over MEDIUM-HOT coals for 7 to 11 minutes or until fish flakes easily with a fork, turning once.

Fresh Corn Cakes:
- 1 batch pancake batter from prepared mix
- 1 ¼ cups fresh corn kernels
- ¾ cup sliced scallions
- ¼ cup chopped green bell pepper
- 2 teaspoons fresh thyme or ½ teaspoon dried
- ¼ teaspoon freshly ground pepper

Fresh Corn Cakes: Mix pancake batter with other ingredients. Heat griddle. When hot lightly oil and pour ¼ cup batter onto griddle. Cook until brown on both sides.

Fish is delicate, so Julia prefers to use a grill basket so it won't fall apart while cooking. This is a tasty combination with the corn cakes, which can be made from a few ears of leftover grilled corn on the cob.

Entrées!
Meat, Poultry & Seafood

Sizzlin' Sausage with Pasta, page 133

Best Beef Stroganoff

Bob Purcell, Athens, Ontario

8 Servings

- 2 pounds round steak, cut into 1-inch cubes
- 1 large onion, chopped
- 1 large green pepper, chopped
- 1 pound fresh mushrooms, whole, halved or sliced
- ½ tablespoon dry mustard powder
- 2 tablespoons Worcestershire sauce
- ½ teaspoon thyme
- ½ teaspoon garlic powder, or to taste
- 1 (8-oz.) package cream cheese

Brown the meat in a large, deep frying pan. Add all the rest of ingredients, turn heat to simmer and cook for 1 hour, covered.

Bob says this recipe is great cooked in a crock pot, too. Serve over mashed potatoes, noodles or rice.

"You don't have to cook fancy or complicated masterpieces — just good food from fresh ingredients."

— *Julia Child*

Entrées — BEEF

Hungarian Goulash

Yvonne Knowles, Freehold, New York

8 Servings

- 3 cups sliced onions
- 1 ½ cups chopped sweet green pepper
- 3 cloves garlic, minced
- 3 pounds beef stew meat, cut into 1-inch cubes
- 1 (6-oz.) can tomato paste
- 4 teaspoons paprika
- ¼ teaspoon each salt and pepper
- 4 cups hot cooked noodles

Garnish:

- ½ cup dairy sour cream

In a 3 ½-quart slow cooker, combine onions, sweet pepper and garlic. Top with meat. In a small bowl combine tomato paste, ½ cup water, paprika, salt and pepper. Pour over meat.

Cover and cook on LOW setting for 10 to 12 hours, or on HIGH setting for 5 or 6 hours. Serve over hot cooked noodles, topped with sour cream, if desired.

Says Yvonne: "I love to use my slow-cooker when I'm camping. I put it on in the morning, enjoy the day, and supper cooks itself!"

Entrées — BEEF

Beef Lyonnaise

Larry Vanzile, Addison, New York

6 Servings

- 16 oz. egg noodles
- ¼ pound margarine or butter, divided
- 2-3 cloves garlic, minced
- 2 sweet green or red peppers (plus 1 hot pepper, optional), coarsely chopped
- 1 large purple onion, peeled and coarsely chopped
- 2 handfuls fresh vegetables of your choice
- 1 pound round steak, sliced into strips ½-inch wide (this works best if slightly frozen)
- ½ cup flour
- Spices of your choice, to taste
- ¾ cup red wine

Larry suggests adding some garlic toast to the table and maybe a glass of that leftover wine for a delicious meal.

Begin boiling water in a large pot for the noodles.

In a large skillet, melt half of margarine, add garlic and cook until golden brown. Add the peppers, onions and other vegetables and cook until they are crunchy-tender. Remove vegetables from the pan and set aside.

Dredge beef strips in the flour mixed with your spices. Melt the remaining margarine in the skillet. Add beef and sauté until completely browned on all sides.

Meanwhile, when the water has come to a boil, add the noodles and cook for about 10 minutes.

Add enough wine to the beef to make a nice sauce. Return the vegetables to the pan to simmer slowly on LOW heat until the noodles are cooked.

Drain the noodles, place on plates and serve the sautéed mixture over the noodles.

Entrées — BEEF

Easy Sloppy Joes
Lynda Mason, Edmonds, Washington

4 Servings

- 1 pound ground beef
- 1 small onion, chopped
- 1 cup catsup
- Chili powder, to taste
- 4 hamburger buns

Lynda says this is very quick and easy — and good!

Brown ground beef with onion. Drain and add catsup and chili powder. Heat thoroughly and serve over hamburger buns.

"If evolution really works, how come mothers only have two hands?"

— *Milton Berle*

Entrées — BEEF

Crock Pot Pork Chops
Linda Stewart, Burleson, Texas

6 Servings

- 6 lean thick-sliced pork tenderloin chops
- 1 box flavored stuffing for pork
- 1 medium onion, sliced thin
- 1 (10-oz.) can cream of onion soup
- ¼ cup water
- Salt and pepper, to taste
- 1 teaspoon poultry seasoning

Place chops in slow cooker that has been sprayed with vegetable oil. Cover with stuffing, then onions. Mix soup with water and pour over top. Add salt, pepper and seasoning. Cook 7 hours on LOW.

Linda suggests substituting cream of mushroom soup and a can of mushrooms instead of the onion soup. Both are good, she says. Add a hot vegetable on the side for a complete meal.

Here's how to bring out the succulent, juicy best in your beef and pork:

Leave a thin layer of fat on steaks, chops and roasts during cooking to seal in juices. Trim fat after cooking. (Fat means flavor.)

Turn steaks, roasts or chops with tongs. Do not use a fork. This pierces the meat and allows flavorful juices to escape.

Turn ground meats with a spatula. Do not flatten patties when cooking. This also allows flavorful juices to escape.

Entrées — PORK

Crock Pot Stuffed Pork Chops

Bonnie Adriance, West Sand Lake, New York

6 Servings

- 6 oz. herb stuffing mix
- 1 cup diced celery
- ½ cup chopped onion
- 6 oz. raisins
- 1 green apple, diced
- ¼ cup butter
- 1 cup chicken broth
- 6 center-cut boneless pork chops

Great served with applesauce and sweet potatoes.

Mix stuffing, vegetables, fruit, butter and broth. Put half of the mixture in a crock pot; add pork chops and remainder of stuffing mixture. Cook on LOW setting for 6-8 hrs.

When cooler weather comes, hot slow-cooked meals are a real favorite with Bonnie's family and friends.

Entrées — PORK

Jamaican Pork and Vegetables
Lisa Rearick, Virginia Beach, Virginia

4 Servings

- 1 gallon-size zipper bag
- 1 pound pork loin roast, cut into 1 ½ inch cubes
- ⅓ cup jerk seasoning
- 1 medium white or yellow onion, quartered
- 1 teaspoon minced garlic
- ⅓ cup sherry
- 1 large sweet potato, peeled and cut into 1 ½ inch cubes
- 1 (4-oz.) jar capers, drained and rinsed

Prepare meat by placing jerk seasoning and meat in zipper bag and tossing to coat. Place onions and garlic in a crock pot and splash on the sherry.

Layer the meat and sweet potato cubes. Cook on LOW for 5-8 hours; add capers the last 20 minutes.

Lisa says this dish can be prepared in a crock pot, or in a dutch oven in the coals or on the stove. If you use a dutch oven, coat the pot generously with oil to prevent the vegetables from sticking.

Pork consumption is highest in the Midwest, followed by the South, the Northeast, and the West. Rural consumers eat more pork than urban/suburban consumers.

— U.S. Department of Agriculture

Sizzlin' Italian Sausage with Pasta

Bob Vance, Yreka, California

4 Servings

- 4 spicy Italian sausages (about 12 ounces), or sausage of your choice
- 2 each red, yellow and green bell peppers (or any combination)
- 1 (22-oz.) can stewed tomatoes
- ½ pound cooked pasta

Garnishes:

- ¼ cup prepared basil pesto

    Grated parmesan cheese

Just a few ingredients are needed for this quick and zesty feast.

Cook sausages until browned. Cut peppers into slices and sauté. Add tomatoes and continue cooking for 15 minutes. Serve over hot pasta, topped with pesto and grated cheese.

How to Avoid Greasy Food:

Always start cooking in a hot skillet. Food won't stick and get greasy from absorbing too-cool oil. When a little oil starts to shimmer and a tiny wisp of smoke appears, the pan is hot enough for cooking.

Entrées — PORK

Stuffed Spudwich
Millie Evans, Agoura, California

4 Servings

- 4 (8-oz.) potatoes
- ½ cup light mayonnaise
- ¼ cup sliced green onions
- ¼ cup sliced celery
- ¼ cup pickle relish
- 2 teaspoons prepared mustard
- ¼ teaspoon pepper
- Salt, to taste
- 4 thin slices cooked ham
- 4 slices Swiss cheese

Pierce potatoes with tines of fork; microwave on HIGH 18 to 20 minutes until potatoes are fork-tender; cool 10 minutes. Halve potatoes and carefully scoop pulp into bowl leaving ¼-inch-thick shells; reserve shells. Mash potato pulp; mix in remaining ingredients except potato shells and ham.

Fill shells with potato mixture. Sandwich 2 halves together with 1 folded ham slice and 1 folded cheese slice in middle. Wrap each spudwich in aluminum foil or a paper napkin to eat out of hand.

Here's a great lunch for picnicking along the road. It combines ham, cheese and potato salad in an easy-to-eat, hand-held "spudwich." Serve with raw vegetables, coleslaw, hard-boiled eggs and brownies for dessert.

"I come from a home where gravy is a beverage."
— Erma Bombeck

Entrées — PORK

Chicken Santa Fe
Diana Baker, Kennewick, Washington

2-4 Servings

- **2-4** boneless, skinless chicken breast halves
- **1** (15-oz.) can kidney or black beans, undrained
- **1** (4-oz.) can sliced jalapeño peppers (optional)
- **1** cup mild or spicy salsa

Preheat oven to 375 F. Place a chicken breast half in the middle of a 10-inch wide piece of aluminum foil (big enough to wrap the meat in with some extra room at the top).

Pour ¼ to ½ of the can of undrained beans on top, add ¼ to ½ of the salsa and optional jalapeños. Join the long ends of the foil above the chicken and fold once or twice, making a tent. Fold up the opposite ends. Repeat with the other chicken breasts.

Put the packets on a flat pan or cookie sheet. Bake in a 375 F oven for approximately 35 minutes.

Diana says to watch out for escaping steam as you open the foil – it's really hot and could burn you! She suggests serving the chicken with rice.

Entrées — CHICKEN

Chicken Piccata

Don and Sandy Lusby, Shediac, New Brunswick

4 Servings

- 2 skinless and boneless whole chicken breasts
- Salt and freshly ground pepper, to taste
- 2 tablespoons olive oil
- ¼ cup white wine
- 2 tablespoons capers, rinsed and drained
- Juice of 1 lemon
- 1 tablespoon butter

Don and Sandy suggest serving this Italian-style chicken with steamed broccoli.

Rinse and pat dry the chicken breasts. Place each breast flat on a chopping board and cut in half. Place each slice between 2 layers of plastic wrap and pound with a mallet until ¼ inch thick. Season each piece with salt and pepper.

To a skillet over HIGH heat, add olive oil and as many of the chicken breast halves as you can fit without crowding. Brown for 2 minutes on each side and then set aside in warm oven.

To make the sauce, reheat the skillet over MEDIUM heat and add the wine and reduce for 2 minutes, stirring to scrape the brown bits off the bottom of the pan. Stir in capers and lemon juice. Remove from heat and add butter. Pour over chicken.

Chicken is now the number one species consumed by Americans and is a descendant of the Southeast Asian red jungle fowl first domesticated in India around 2000 B.C.

— *U.S. Department of Agriculture*

Filipino Chicken Adobo
Cathy Kelly, Terry, Mississippi

4-6 Servings

- 1 pound boneless, skinless chicken breasts, cut into bite-size pieces
- ½ cup soy sauce
- ½ cup balsamic vinegar
- 1 ½ teaspoons crushed garlic
- Pepper, to taste
- 1 small bay leaf

Adobo is the national dish of the Phillipines. It is typically made with a generous amount of garlic and white or rice wine vinegar. Cathy has adapted the recipe with a few changes of her own. Serve hot with rice.

Mix all ingredients in a pot and marinate for about 5 minutes. Bring to a boil, then lower heat to a simmer and cook covered without stirring until meat is almost cooked, about 30 minutes. Remove cover, stir and continue simmering until meat is tender.

Nacho Chicken Delight
Carlene Stewart, Grimes, Iowa

4 Servings

- 4 tablespoons mayonnaise
- ⅓ teaspoon salt
- ½ teaspoon Italian seasoning
- 4 skinless, boneless chicken breast halves
- 1 cup nacho cheese-flavored tortilla chips
- 1 tablespoon butter or margarine, melted

Preheat oven to 350 F. Grease bottom of 9x13-inch baking pan. Combine mayonnaise, salt and Italian seasoning. Spread on both sides of chicken. Roll chicken in crushed chips and place in baking pan. Drizzle with melted butter. Bake at 350 F for 20-25 minutes or until chicken is done.

Line the baking pan with aluminum foil or an oven-roasting bag to eliminate messy cleanup after dinner.

Entrées — CHICKEN

Skillet Barbecued Chicken Breasts

Judy Coros, Granger, Indiana

4 Servings

- 4 boneless, skinless chicken breast halves
- Cooking oil, as needed
- Onions to taste, sliced or chopped
- 1 cup catsup
- 1 (12-oz.) can cola

Judy suggests that if you like thick barbecue sauce use less cola, and if you want a low-calorie dish use diet cola.

Cook the chicken breasts in a skillet with oil and onions. When they are just done, add the catsup and cola.

Chicken Livers in Sherry

Bill Graves, *Trailer Life* columnist, Rancho Palos Verdes, California

4 Servings

- 1 pound chicken livers
- Flour, salt and pepper
- ¼ pound butter or margarine
- 1 clove garlic, sliced, or use dried minced garlic if that is all you have
- ½ cup sherry
- Lemon juice, if desired

Dip and roll chicken livers in some flour, mixed with salt and pepper. Fry very lightly in hot butter or butter substitute with the garlic. Do not overcook. When butter has been used up, add the sherry and swish around in the pan over a hot fire until the sherry is absorbed.

Bill serves this dish with rice or rye bread, with a squeeze of lemon juice.

Entrées — CHICKEN

Pacific Rim Pecan Crusted Turkey Cutlets

Margee Berry, White Salmon, Washington

6 Servings

- ¼ cup hoisin sauce
- 2 tablespoons soy sauce
- 1 tablespoon sesame oil
- 1 tablespoon seasoned rice vinegar
- 1 teaspoon liquid hot sauce
- ¼ teaspoon ground ginger
- 2 cups finely ground pecans
- 6 turkey cutlets
- 12 ounces ramen noodles

Preheat broiler and grease broiler rack. In a shallow bowl, mix together the hoisin sauce, soy sauce, sesame oil, rice vinegar, hot sauce and ginger. Place pecans on wax paper. Dip each turkey cutlet into the liquid mixture and then into the pecans, pressing so the pecans stick. Place on broiler-pan rack. Broil 6 inches from heat, 3-4 minutes per side.

While cutlets are cooking, transfer remaining liquid mixture to a saucepan and bring to boil. Lower heat and keep liquid warm over LOW heat. Cook the ramen noodles without the seasoning pack according to package directions. To serve, place ramen noodles onto six dinner plates, then top each serving with a cutlet and drizzle with warmed sauce.

Margie won second place in the "I Can Use Pecans in That?" recipe contest with this dish.

"Cuisine is just fine, but there are times when food is better."

— *unknown*

Entrées — TURKEY

Oven-Barbecued Turkey

Bill O'Bier, Richmond, Virginia

Serves a Crowd

- 1 5-7 pound frozen turkey breast, thawed
- 2 bottles of your favorite barbeque sauce (add more or less sauce, depending on the amount of turkey)

    Hot sauce, to your taste (optional)

Toppings (if desired):

Coleslaw

Chopped onions

Pulled roasted turkey breast replaces pork in this updated version.

Place thawed turkey breast in roasting pan. Cover with lid (or aluminum foil). Roast in a 325 F oven for 2 to 2 ½ hours until a meat thermometer reaches 170 F.

After roasting, allow the turkey breast to cool. Hand-pull all the meat into shreds and place in a crock-pot slow cooker (4-quart). Add the barbeque sauce and hot sauce and mix well. Place crock pot on LOW setting and warm 2-3 hours until all flavors are mixed. Serve with toppings.

Traditions That Work!

Certain herbal plants with aromatic oils aid in the digestion of fatty food, and have become traditional accompaniments to dishes. So we serve mint with lamb, sage with pork and horseradish with beef, not just because the flavors complement each other, but because they help us digest the meat. Cranberries may help us with that Thanksgiving turkey, and ginger is also helpful with almost anything.

Entrées — TURKEY

Stuffed Sole

Chuck Campbell, *Trailer Life* and *MotorHome* columnist, Thousand Oaks, CA

4 Servings

- ¼ cup butter
- ¼ cup finely chopped green onion or white onion
- 1 (3-oz.) can chopped mushrooms; reserve liquid
- 1 (7-oz.) can crabmeat, drained well
- 1 (7-oz.) can small shrimp, drained well
- ½ cup saltine crackers, coarsely chopped
- 2 tablespoons fresh parsley, snipped
- ½ teaspoon salt
- Dash pepper
- 2 pounds Dover sole fillets, medium-size
- 3 tablespoons butter
- 3 tablespoons flour
- 1 to 1 ¼ cups milk (depends on amount of mushroom liquid)
- ⅓ cup sherry or dry white wine
- 1 cup shredded Swiss cheese
- ½ teaspoon paprika

Stuffing: In skillet, sauté onion in ¼ cup butter until tender. Drain mushrooms and set liquid aside. Chop mushrooms into smaller bits. Add to sautéed onions in skillet along with crabmeat, shrimp, cracker crumbs, parsley, salt and pepper. Toss lightly together, and set aside to cool a bit.

Lightly spray cooking oil in an 11x7x2-inch baking dish. Rinse sole fillets and blot dry with paper towels. Take the fillets one at a time, set inside dish, and drop in one generous tablespoon of stuffing mixture. Roll up snugly with seam side down, attempting to keep as much stuffing inside as possible. Place rolls shoulder-to-shoulder in rows, and continue until all stuffing and fillets are used.

Sauce: In medium saucepan, melt butter. Slowly blend in flour. Add enough milk to reserved mushroom liquid to make 1 ½ cups of liquid. Add liquid and wine to saucepan. Cook over MEDIUM heat and stir constantly with whisk until mixture thickens and bubbles. Pour over stuffed fillets.

Bake stuffed fillets at 400 F for 25 minutes. Remove from oven, sprinkle with shredded cheese, dust with paprika, and return about 10 minutes longer. When done, fish should flake when tested with fork.

Chuck says use green onions and sherry for a richer flavor.

Serve the stuffed fillets with long-grain and wild-rice pilaf, salad and hot French bread.

Entrées — SEAFOOD

Linguine with White Clam Sauce

David Hinchcliffe, Albuquerque, New Mexico

4 Servings

- 1 (10-oz.) can whole baby clams, not drained, or 10 oz. frozen, with shells (optional)
- 2 tablespoons light butter
- 1 tablespoon olive oil
- 3 cloves garlic, minced
- 1 tablespoon all-purpose flour
- ½ cup dry white wine
- 2 tablespoons chopped fresh parsley
- 1 teaspoon chopped fresh thyme
- ⅛ teaspoon pepper
- 1 (6.5-oz.) can minced clams, drained
- 4 cups hot cooked linguine (about 8 oz. uncooked pasta)

Garnish:

Thyme sprigs (optional)

Drain baby clams in a sieve over a bowl, reserving juice. Heat butter and olive oil in a medium saucepan over medium heat. Add garlic and sauté 1 minute.

Stir in flour. Stir in the reserved clam juice, wine, chopped parsley, chopped thyme and pepper, and cook 2 minutes, stirring frequently.

Add the baby clams and the minced clams, and cook 3 minutes or until thoroughly heated. Serve clam sauce over pasta. Garnish with thyme sprigs, if desired.

Always a favorite, this pasta dish owes its flavor to garlic, wine and fresh herbs.

Entrées — SEAFOOD

Thadd's Shellfish Pasta Mess

Thadd and Lindy McNamara, Rollling Hills Estates, California

4 Servings

- ½ pound angel hair or bow tie pasta
- ½ pound frozen shellfish (calamari, shrimps, scallops, clams)
- ¼ pound frozen wild mushrooms
- Extra-virgin olive oil
- Garlic, minced
- 2 tablespoons capers, drained and rinsed
- Kosher salt, cracked pepper, seafood seasoning blend, red pepper flakes, to taste
- A splash of sherry (optional)
- ¼ cup sour cream

Serve in individual bowls with a crisp white wine and lots of crusty French bread and butter. A fresh salad goes well with it.

Thadd says: "We keep bags of assorted frozen shellfish and exotic mushrooms in our freezer because they are small, keep well and are something that you rarely find out in the wilds. We generally stock up on them on our visits to Trader Joe's markets. This recipe is tasty, fast, and filling. Try it; you will love it — as will your guests."

Saute the shellfish and mushrooms in the oil with the onion, garlic and capers. Add seasonings and sherry to taste.

While this sautéing is going on, heat water for the pasta. When it boils, add the pasta and cook 9 minutes.

About the time the pasta is ready, add the sour cream to the sauté mixture, drain the pasta, and toss the whole mess together.

Entrées — SEAFOOD

Allegheny Al's Perch Patties

Allegheny Al, Erie, Pennsylvania

4 Servings

- 1 pound fresh or frozen perch fillets
- 1 egg
- Onion, chopped, to taste
- ½ cup flour
- Salt and pepper, to taste
- Oil for frying

According to Al, these patties don't take long to cook because after parboiling the fish you are just browning the patties.

Thaw the perch if frozen. Bring a pan of water to the boil and place perch fillets into the boiling water for no more than two minutes. Immediately drain off hot water and plunge the fish into a pan of cold water. Let cool.

In a bowl, break fillets into little pieces. Add egg, chopped onion, flour and seasoning. Mix well and form into patties. Heat ⅛ inch of oil in a pan, add patties and brown each side to a golden brown.

This is good for any mild fish, so Al suggests you experiment with any fish you like.

Tip

Freezing Fish

Shara Wright, Midland, Texas

This Tip works with raw chicken breasts too!

To freeze your fresh fillets, place fillets of fish in freezer baggies and fill with enough water to cover the fish. Allow room for the water to expand as it freezes, and press out air pockets. Seal well and label, then freeze.

To thaw, place baggie in sink or pan filled with cool water. It will thaw within the hour and you will not be able to tell it was ever frozen! The best thing is that due to the water surrounding and protecting the meat, it will never get freezer burn!

Entrées — SEAFOOD

Side Dishes!

Easy Potato Pancakes, page 148

Potato Pesto Bake

Greg Rozman, St. Louis, Missouri

6 Servings

- 1 teaspoon butter or margarine, softened
- 4 cups frozen shredded hash brown potatoes, divided
- ½ cup prepared pesto
- 1 cup shredded cheese of your choice
- 1 cup milk
- ¼ cup shredded parmesan cheese
- ½ teaspoon pepper
- ¼ teaspoon salt

Topping:

- 2 tablespoons butter or margarine, softened
- ⅓ cup Italian-style bread crumbs
- ⅓ cup shredded parmesan cheese

Heat oven to 425 F. Lightly grease 11x7-inch baking dish with 1 teaspoon of butter. Place 2 cups of the shredded potatoes in prepared dish, pressing lightly to form an even layer. Dollop pesto over potatoes; sprinkle with shredded cheese. Top with remaining 2 cups potatoes, spreading evenly.

In medium microwave-safe dish, microwave milk on HIGH for 1 ½ to 2 minutes or until hot; stir in ¼ cup parmesan cheese, pepper and salt. Pour over potatoes.

In small bowl, mix together topping ingredients until blended; sprinkle over potatoes. Bake, uncovered, 23 to 25 minutes or until top is crisp and browned. Let stand 5 minutes before serving.

Here's yet another way to use convenient frozen potatoes. Greg's casserole is full of texture and the flavors of basil pesto and cheese.

"The potato, like man, was not meant to dwell alone."

— *Shila Hibbe*

Side Dishes

Renie's Cheesy Potatoes & Onions

Renie Willingham, Brinkley, Arkansas

4 Servings

- **4-5** medium red potatoes
- **3** Vidalia sweet onions, chopped
- Garlic powder and cayenne pepper, to taste
- **½** (10 ½-oz.) can chicken broth
- **½** cup shredded cheddar, pepper jack or any combination
- **1** jalapeño pepper, chopped (optional)

Wash and cut potatoes into cubes, leaving the peel on. Spray a covered microwaveable dish with oil and add potatoes, onions, garlic powder and cayenne pepper. Add just enough chicken broth to cover the bottom of the dish. Cover and microwave for 20 minutes.

Top with cheese and jalapeño. Cover and cook another 5 to 10 minutes, or until cheese is melted.

This is so easy, says Renie, and it goes great with any meat or just makes the basis of a tasty all-vegetable supper.

Side Dishes

Low-Fat Mashed Potatoes
Connie Stallworth, Smyrna, Georgia

4 Servings

- 1-2 potatoes per person
- 1 (10 ½-oz.) can low-fat chicken broth
- Salt and pepper, to taste

Peel and cut up the desired amount of potatoes and boil in water till tender. Then whip with broth. Add salt and pepper.

Connie cautions: "Use low-fat chicken broth in place of cream. The dish is almost fat-free and low in calories. Just remember, potatoes are still carbs!"

Easy Potato Pancakes
Heather and Ed Rodger, Kelowna, British Columbia

4 Servings

- 1 batch pancake batter (use prepared mix or your own recipe)
- Hash browns (frozen, thawed) to taste
- Chopped onion (optional)

Garnishes:
- Sour cream, butter, applesauce, syrup, bacon as desired

Make pancake batter according to box directions or your own recipe. Add thawed hash browns — enough to make the batter medium-thick — and onion if desired. Fry as usual and drain on paper towels.

This is a shortcut version that eliminates grating raw potatoes. Serve with sour cream, butter, applesauce, syrup, bacon or all of the above.

Corn Pudding
Susan Young, Junction City, Oregon

2 Servings

- 1 egg
- ½ cup milk
- 1 tablespoon sugar
- 1 (14 ½-oz.) can cream-style corn
- ¾ cup crushed saltine crackers
- 2 tablespoons butter, cut in pieces
- Paprika, to taste
- Chopped green pepper or bacon pieces (optional)

Place egg in 1 ½-quart casserole dish and beat well with fork. Stir in milk, sugar, corn, crackers and butter. Microwave at MEDIUM-HIGH for 7 minutes. Stir well, sprinkle with paprika. Microwave another 11-14 minutes. Top with sautéed green pepper or cooked bacon pieces, if desired.

This microwaved dish resembles Southern spoon bread. When done, the center will be just barely set.

Easy Applesauce
Larry, Santa Clara, California

Peel and cut up enough apples to fill a crock pot. Pour one (12-oz.) can of 7-Up over the apple pieces, add cinnamon to taste and cook on low heat for several hours.

Side Dishes

150 RV Trail Beans

Chuck Campbell, *Trailer Life* and *MotorHome* columnist, Thousand Oaks, CA

4 Servings

- 1 (28-oz.) can pork and beans
- 4-6 slices bacon
- ½ cup onion, coarsely chopped
- 2 cloves garlic, minced
- 2 tablespoons catsup
- 2 tablespoons brown sugar
- Hot sauce
- Dash liquid smoke

Fry bacon in pan until limp, but not crisp. Set aside bacon to drain on paper towels, and chop into small pieces when cool enough. Sautée onion in bacon grease until nearly tender, then add garlic for a few minutes more. Drain onion-garlic mixture with a slotted spoon onto a paper towel.

Place beans in large saucepan. Add bacon pieces, sautéed onion and garlic, catsup, brown sugar and a dash of hot sauce. Add several dashes or more of liquid smoke, to taste. Warm bean mixture over MEDIUM heat until bubbling, stirring occasionally.

This recipe makes a quick and easy accompaniment for barbequed meats such as steaks, tri-tip or chicken, Chuck tells us.

Many fresh vegetables taste great when grilled.

If using skewers, put one kind of vegetable on each skewer so you can control cooking; mixed vegetable and meat kabobs look great but it's difficult to get everything done at the same time.

Double-pronged skewers secure the pieces so they can't spin around and are less likely to crack and drop off.

Side Dishes

Sweet 'n' Salty Baked-Bean Medley

Lisa Rearick, Virginia Beach, Virginia

8 Servings

- 1 (14 ½-oz.) can of your favorite prepared baked beans
- 1 (14 ½-oz.) can green beans, drained
- 1 (14 ½-oz.) can kidney beans, rinsed and drained
- 1 (14 ½-oz.) can butter beans, rinsed and drained
- 1 medium onion, chopped medium
- ⅓ cup prepared mustard
- ½ cup honey or maple syrup
- 1 pound bacon, cooked and crumbled

Mix all ingredients in a large dutch oven or crock pot. Cover and cook on LOW for about 4 hours.

Lisa says this goes great with Southern barbecue dishes.

"Like all great travelers, I have seen more than I remember and remember more than I have seen."

— *Benjamin Disraeli*

Side Dishes

Ratatouille Rice

Jeannette Nagel, Sun City West, Arizona

- 1 tablespoon olive oil
- 1 medium-size onion, chopped
- 3 cloves garlic, minced or pressed
- ½ pound sliced fresh mushrooms
- 1 small (¾ pound) eggplant, unpeeled and cut into ½-inch cubes
- 1 large green pepper, seeded and chopped
- 1 (15-oz.) can tomato sauce
- 1 cup chicken broth
- 1 ½ teaspoons dry thyme
- 1 ½ cups brown rice
- 1 small can sliced black olives (optional)

Heat oil in a large frying pan over MEDIUM heat. Cook onion until soft. Add in garlic and cook for one minute. Add mushrooms, eggplant and bell pepper. Stir until all liquid has evaporated.

Place the vegetable mixture into a 3-4 quart casserole dish. Add in the tomato sauce, broth, thyme and rice and mix together. Cover and bake at 350 F for about 1 hour (until the rice is tender). Mix in olives if desired and let sit for 5 minutes.

The popular French "stew" is rethought, mixed with rice and baked in a casserole.

"I want my children to have all the things I couldn't afford. Then I want to move in with them."

— *Phyllis Diller*

Side Dishes

Easiest One-Pan Spanish Rice

Pat Allen, Cocoa Beach, Florida

2-4 Servings

- 4 slices bacon or ½ pound ground beef, turkey or lamb
- 1 medium onion, chopped, sliced or diced
- 1 cup quick-cooking rice
- 1 cup tomato sauce
- 1 cup water
- ¼ teaspoon black pepper
- ¼ teaspoon garlic powder
- ¼ teaspoon chili powder

This is a quick and easy recipe that can be cooked in a cast-iron skillet over an open campfire, in any pot over a camp stove, or in a non-stick frying pan in the comfort of your RV. Any type of meat, any combination of vegetables (see notes), any type of cooking pot will do. And the best part is there's only one pot to clean when the meal is over.

In a large skillet, over MEDIUM-HIGH heat, cook bacon until nicely browned and crisp. Remove bacon to paper towel to drain; crumble when cool.

Meanwhile, remove all but 2 teaspoons of drippings from pan, add onion and cook until translucent. Add rice, mix well with onion, and continue cooking for 2 minutes. Add tomato sauce, water and seasonings.

Reduce heat to medium-low and cook, uncovered, stirring occasionally, until all liquid is absorbed. Add crumbled bacon, stir and serve.

Notes: This recipe can easily be doubled, tripled, etc. to serve as many as needed. Just be sure to use a sufficiently large pan to accommodate the quantity of rice being used.

Substitute any ground meat for the bacon — or go meatless, if you wish. Just be sure to use sufficient cooking oil to prevent the meat from sticking, and retain 2 teaspoons of the cooking oil to cook the onion.

Experiment to find the combination of ingredients that best suits your taste. Try adding green, red, and/or yellow bell peppers, zucchini and/or yellow squash, green onions or hot peppers.

Side Dishes

Spinach-Stuffed Tomatoes

Sue Bray, Executive Director, Good Sam Club, Thousand Oaks, California

- 4 medium tomatoes
- ½ tablespoon olive oil or salad oil
- 1 small onion – chopped
- ½ pound cleaned spinach, coarsely chopped
- ¼ cup dry bread crumbs (Italian style is extra good)
- ¼ cup grated parmesan cheese
- ⅛ teaspoon ground nutmeg

Fancy enough for company, easy enough for every day.

Cut off the top ¼ of each tomato. (Save this for use later in a salad or salsa.) Scoop out the pulp and seeds to make hollow shells. Chop the pulp and let drain on a paper towel.

Heat oil in a large frying pan over MEDIUM heat. Add onion and cook until soft, about 6 or 7 minutes. Stir in drained tomato pulp and spinach. Cook about 3 minutes. Stir in bread crumbs, 2 tablespoons of cheese and the nutmeg.

Fill the tomatoes with the spinach mixture and place in an ungreased baking pan. Sprinkle with remaining cheese. Broil about 4 inches below the heat until the cheese is lightly browned. If you are in your RV and can't broil, bake for about 5 minutes at 375 F.

If you are refrigerating your tomatoes, you are not allowing them to ripen and are actually ruining their tomato flavor. For tomatoes to ripen fully, they should be stored at temperatures between 55-65 F.

— California Tomato Commission

Side Dishes

Grilled Artichokes
California Artichoke Advisory Board

8 Servings

- 4 large artichokes
- ¼ cup balsamic vinegar
- ¼ cup water
- ¼ cup soy sauce
- 1 tablespoon minced ginger
- ¼ cup olive oil

This recipe is perfect for the lazy cook, since all preparation can be done the previous day. The slightly smoky taste compliments the nuttiness of the artichoke and no dip is necessary, although some might want to use additional marinade for dipping.

Slice artichoke tops off, crosswise. Trim stems. Boil or steam artichokes until bottoms pierce easily, or a petal pulls off easily. Drain artichokes. Cool. Cut each artichoke in half lengthwise and scrape out fuzzy center and any purple tipped petals.

Mix remaining ingredients in a large plastic bag. Place artichokes in the bag and coat all sides of the artichokes. For best flavor marinate in the mixture overnight in the refrigerator, or at least one hour.

Drain artichokes. Place cut side down on a grill over a solid bed of MEDIUM coals or gas grill on MEDIUM. Grill until lightly browned on the cut side, 5 to 7 minutes. Turn artichokes over and drizzle some of the remaining marinade over the artichokes. Grill until petal tips are lightly charred, 3 to 4 minutes more. Serve hot or room temperature.

"I know I'm drinking myself to a slow death, but then I'm in no hurry."
— *Robert Benchley*

Side Dishes

Asparagus Tapas with Red Pepper Sauce

California Asparagus Commission

4 Servings

- 2 large red bell peppers, cored and seeded
- 2 cloves garlic, minced
- 1 tablespoon olive oil
- 2 tablespoons raspberry vinegar
- 1 ½ tablespoons chopped fresh basil
- ½ teaspoon salt freshly ground pepper
- 1 pound fresh asparagus, trimmed
- 1 sourdough or French baguette loaf

Garnishes:

- Sliced julienne strips of bell pepper
- Snipped fresh basil
- Shaved parmesan cheese

Coarsely chop bell peppers. Heat olive oil in a large skillet. Add peppers and garlic; cook over MEDIUM heat for about 15 minutes or until peppers are softened, stirring occasionally.

Remove from heat and let cool slightly. Place in blender or food processor and puree until smooth; stir in vinegar, basil, salt and pepper. Cook asparagus spears in boiling salted water for 4 to 5 minutes until crisp-tender; drain.

Spoon red pepper sauce on a platter and arrange asparagus over sauce. Garnish with bell pepper, basil and parmesan, if desired. Serve with baguette slices.

Tapas are defined as complimentary snacks or hors d'ouevres served at a Spanish bar. This one makes an unusual side dish to serve with any entrée.

> *"Poverty is not a disgrace, but it's terribly inconvenient."*
>
> — *Milton Berle*

Foil-Roasted Herb Onion Bloom
National Onion Association

1 Serving

- 1 large onion (3 – 3 ½ inches wide)
- 1 tablespoon butter or margarine
- 1 teaspoon dried thyme or oregano
- ½ teaspoon dried rosemary
- Salt and pepper, to taste

Garnishes (optional):
- Parsley, minced
- Paprika

Roast this on the grill while you are cooking other food, or bake in the oven.

Cut about ½-inch off top of onion; peel onion. Cut onion into 12 to 16 vertical wedges, leaving root base intact. Set bloomed onion on 14x10-inch foil piece. Top onion with butter, thyme or oregano, rosemary and salt and pepper, to taste.

Wrap foil around seasoned bloom and pinch edges together tightly. Put on MEDIUM grill or placed wrapped onion upright on a pan and bake at 425 F for 30 minutes, or until tender and cooked but "petals" still have body and stand upright. If desired, sprinkle with minced parsley or paprika. Baked wrapped onion may be held in warm location for up to 1 hour before serving.

Side Dishes

Pineapple Casserole

Carol Smith, Largo, Florida

4 Servings

- 1 (20-oz.) can pineapple chunks in juice, drained (reserve 3 tablespoons juice)
- ½ cup sugar
- 3 tablespoons all-purpose flour
- 1 cup cheddar cheese, shredded
- 1 cup buttery cracker crumbs
- 3 tablespoons melted butter or margarine

Combine sugar and flour; stir in reserved pineapple juice. Stir in cheese and pineapple chunks. Spoon mixture into a greased 1-quart casserole dish. Combine cracker crumbs and butter, stirring well. Sprinkle over pineapple mixture. Bake, uncovered at 350 F for 25 - 30 minutes or until browned.

Although fruit is often served as a condiment or garnish with a main course, this fancy dish goes particularly well with ham or chicken.

Roasted Garlic

Roast garlic on the grill when you are cooking any meal and keep some for later. Add to spreads, soups and sauces, or use as is to spread on warm crusty bread.

Take a head of garlic, remove the skin but leave the root intact, and slice ½ inch off the top. Center the garlic head on a 10-inch square of foil. Pour 1 teaspoon of olive oil over the head and wrap the foil around it. Roast until the cloves are soft and the top is golden, 35-45 minutes on a MEDIUM-HIGH to HIGH grill.

Allow the packet to cool for about 10 minutes. Unwrap the garlic and let it sit until the cloves are cool enough to handle. Separate the cloves and gently squeeze the narrow end to remove the cloves from the tough skin.

Side Dishes

Desserts!

All-American Apricot Lattice Pie, page 175

Chocolate Fondue & Dippers
Barbara Adams, Scotts Valley, California

8 Servings

- 1 (12-oz.) can evaporated milk
- 1 (12-oz.) package semi-sweet chocolate chips
- 1 teaspoon vanilla extract

Dippers (your choice):
- **Banana slices**
- **Pineapple chunks**
- **Whole strawberries**
- **Apple slices**
- **Kiwi fruit**
- **Pear slices**
- **Orange sections**
- **Pound cake cubes**
- **Biscotti**
- **Marshmallows**

Probably the easiest dessert recipe ever developed.

Prepare the dippers: Wash, peel and cut the fruit into bite-size pieces. Arrange the fruit, cake, biscotti and/or marshmallows on a platter. If using apples or bananas, squirt them with lemon juice so they won't turn brown. Cover the platter and set it aside.

Combine the evaporated milk and chocolate chips in a heavy-duty saucepan or a metal bowl placed over a pot of boiling water to make a double boiler. Cook over LOW heat, stirring, until the chips are melted. Remove from the heat and stir in the vanilla extract.

Serve in a fondue pot or microwaveable dish. If the chocolate cools, heat it in the microwave for 1-2 minutes.

Pots de Crème au Chocolat

Phyllis Gordon, Henderson, Nevada

6 Servings

- 1 cup semi-sweet chocolate chips
- 1 ½ cups half-and-half, scalded
- 2 egg yolks
- 3 tablespoons brandy, orange liquor, rum, whiskey or coffee
- Whipped cream

Mix all ingredients well in blender. Place in pots de crème or demitasse cups, small ramekins or custard cups. Chill several hours or overnight. To serve, top with whipped cream.

The half-and-half needs to be very hot to cook the egg yolks safely.

Almond-Amaretto Truffles

Jean Scott, Newbury Park, California

30 Pieces

- 1 (11 ½-oz.) package (2 cups) semi-sweet chocolate chips
- ¼ cup sour cream
- ⅔ cup finely chopped toasted almonds
- 2 tablespoons almond flavored (amaretto) liqueur

Melt chips over hot (not boiling) water. Stir until smooth. Remove from heat and blend in sour cream. Add almond liqueur, mix well. Transfer to small bowl and chill until firm. Drop by rounded teaspoonfuls onto waxed paper-lined cookie sheets. Shape into balls. Roll in almonds. Chill until firm, about 30 minutes.

These confections are perfect for an elegant adult dinner.

Desserts

Graham Cracker Pudding
Cathy Dubois, Weston, Ohio

8 Servings

- 14 graham crackers
- 2 cups milk
- ½ cup sugar
- 3 egg yolks
- Pinch of salt
- 2 tablespoons butter
- 2 tablespoons cornstarch
- 1 tablespoon flour
- 4 bananas, sliced

Crush the crackers. Mix a couple of spoonfuls of the milk with the cornstarch and set aside. Make a custard of the remaining ingredients. When it is almost to a boil, stir in the starch mixture and continue to cook on LOW heat, stirring, until thick.

In a large baking dish, put a layer of the custard, a layer of the sliced bananas, and a layer of the cracker crumbs. Continue to make layers until the ingredients are all used up. Chill for several hours or overnight.

Cathy's recipe resembles banana-cream pie — with the crumb crust on the inside!

Say "No!" to Burned Bottoms
Kathleen Waldron, Modesto, California

I was having a terrible time baking biscuits, brownies, etc. in my RV oven without burning the bottoms. I had tried all the other suggestions that I had read and heard about, but nothing worked as well as the solution my Aunt Nae shared with me: Air-bake pans (with a layer of air between two sheets of metal) are wonderful. I no longer worry about baking in my RV oven; everything turns out perfect every time.

Desserts

Chocolate Yogurt Pudding

Lissa Ellingston, Vallejo, California

4 Servings

- 1 (4-serving) package instant pudding mix
- 2 cups non-fat plain yogurt

Mix and chill.

Lissa says this tastes like chocolate cheesecake, only better. She uses no-fat, no-sugar pudding mix.

Green Dream Dessert

Julie Hoy, Langhome, Pennsylvania

8 Servings

- 1 can crushed pineapple (do not drain)
- 1 (4-serving) box pistachio pudding mix
- 1 (8-oz.) tub frozen topping (may use low-fat)
- 1 bag mini marshmallows

Garnish:

Maraschino cherries

Place pineapple in large mixing bowl, sprinkle with dry pudding mix. Stir to combine. Stir in topping and add marshmallows. Use cherries to garnish. Put in refrigerator and serve chilled.

Sit back and watch it disappear!

Desserts

Lemon Panna Cotta with Raspberry-Orange Sauce

Sandy Lusby, Shediac, New Brunswick

8 Servings

- 3 cups heavy cream
- ½ cup sugar
- 1 ½ teaspoons lemon zest, grated very fine
- 1 oz. unflavored gelatin
- 4 tablespoons orange-flavored liqueur, divided
- 1 (12-oz.) package frozen strawberries
- 6 oz. fresh raspberries

Bring cream, sugar and lemon zest to a simmer in a large saucepan over MEDIUM-LOW heat. Meanwhile, in a small bowl, soften the gelatin in 2 generous tablespoons of cold water until dissolved. Whisk softened gelatin and 2 tablespoons of orange liqueur into the cream mixture.

Spray 8 (4-oz.) ramekins or custard cups lightly with vegetable cooking spray. Blot excess oil with a paper towel. Pour cream mixture into cups. Set in a shallow pan, cover with plastic wrap and refrigerate until set — at least 4 hours, but best overnight.

Partially thaw strawberries at room temperature. Place in a food processor fitted with a metal blade and add remaining sugar and 2 tablespoons orange liqueur. Transfer sauce to a medium bowl. (For a seedless sauce, strain through a fine sieve.) Stir in fresh raspberries and let stand about 1 hour.

When ready to serve, run a knife around each dessert to loosen. Turn onto a dessert plate and spoon raspberry sauce around it. If you freeze the cups, allow 20 minutes to thaw before serving.

This dessert is silky-smooth. Sandy says it freezes well and is easy to make.

Desserts

Light, Lemony and Luscious Dessert

Sandy Lusby, Shediac, New Brunswick

Crust:

- 1 cup graham wafer crumbs
- 3 tablespoon butter, melted
- 2 tablespoons granulated sugar

Filling:

- 1 (3-oz.) package lemon gelatin dessert powder
- 1 cup boiling water
- ⅔ cup fat-free evaporated milk
- 1 (8-oz.) package light cream cheese, softened
- ¼ cup granulated sugar

Garnish:

- Fresh fruit of your choice

Another wonderful dessert from Sandy; plus she says it is easy to make.

Combine wafer crumbs, butter and sugar in small bowl; set aside 1 tablespoon of crumb mixture for topping. Press remaining crumb mixture into bottom of 8-inch square baking dish.

Place gelatin powder in bowl; stir in water until dissolved. Let cool to room temperature.

Pour evaporated milk into a small bowl. Chill in freezer 15-20 minutes or until ice crystals form around edge.

Beat together cream cheese and sugar in large bowl. Gradually beat in cooled gelatin until combined.

Using clean beaters, beat chilled evaporated milk 1 minute or until stiff; fold into cream-cheese mixture. Pour over crumb crust. Sprinkle with reserved crumbs. Chill until set. Garnish with fresh fruit, if desired.

"People want economy and will pay any price to get it."

— Lee Iacocca

Scotcharoos

Charlotte Barnett, Arlington, Texas

6 Servings

- 1 cup sugar (part brown sugar, if you like)
- 1 cup corn syrup
- Dash salt
- 1 cup peanut butter
- 6 cups of crispy rice cereal (part cocoa flavored, if you like)

Boil sugar, corn syrup and salt for 1 minute. Remove from heat.

Stir in peanut butter and cereal.

Pour into a buttered pan or flat plastic storage container. Cool and cut or break into pieces.

These are a no-bake treat. You can also add a 12-oz. package of chocolate chips or butterscotch chips, or ½ package of each!

Low-Fat Frozen Treats

Jean Godfrey, Calera, Alabama

Feeds a Crowd

- Low-fat dessert topping
- Low-fat graham crackers

Break graham cracker in half and place a blob of topping between two halves. Prepare several and place on cookie sheet in freezer.

After 30 minutes take them out, place in a freezer bag and put them back — if you can resist eating them immediately!

Jean says when you need a sweet fix, just reach into the freezer and get one. Try it with chocolate-coated graham crackers.

Desserts

Armpit Fudge

Nancy Emery, Waterford, Michigan

167

1-8 Servings

Single-serving version:

- 2 oz. powdered sugar (½ cup)
- 1 tablespoon butter
- 2 teaspoons cream cheese
- Dash vanilla
- 2 teaspoons cocoa powder

Options:

Raisins, chocolate-coated candies, peanut butter, chopped nuts

"Patrol-size" version:

- 1 pound powdered sugar
- ¼ cup butter
- 1 (3-oz.) package cream cheese
- ½ teaspoon vanilla
- ⅓ cup cocoa powder

Options:

Raisins, chocolate-coated candies, peanut butter, chopped nuts

Single-serving version: place all ingredients in a sandwich-size plastic resealable bag. Squeeze out all the air. Squish and moosh the bag (under the arm!) until all the ingredients are well mixed and the fudge has a creamy consistency. Take out a spoon and enjoy.

Or try the "patrol-size" version: mix the ingredients in a one-gallon resealable bag. Pass from person to person until it's all blended together.

This is one of Nancy's favorite Girl Scout recipes. It sounds strange, but is delicious. She made it last summer while camping with her sisters and their daughters and everyone loved it.

Desserts

Chocolate-Oatmeal-Peanut Butter No-Bake Cookies

Pat Robinson, Annapolis, Maryland

36 Cookies

- 4 ounces butter or margarine
- ½ cup milk
- 2 cups sugar
- 1 cup semi-sweet chocolate chips
- 3 to 4 tablespoons peanut butter, optional
- 3 cups oats, quick or old-fashioned
- 1 teaspoon vanilla extract

Place chocolate chips, peanut butter (if used), oats and vanilla in a large mixing bowl.

Combine the butter or margarine, milk and sugar in a saucepan; bring to a rolling boil. Boil for 1 minute. Combine the hot mixture with the oatmeal and chocolate chip mixture; stir well. Drop by spoonfuls onto waxed paper. Chill until firm.

Chocolate, peanut butter and oats — who doesn't like this combination?

Floor Tile in the Oven?!

A recent discussion on the Open Roads Forum on rv.net dealt with using of floor tiles in the oven to keep foods from browning too quickly. Participants recommended both glazed and non-glazed floor tiles, large or small, placed on the floor of the oven or on the rack with the pan on top. Some suggested using a pizza stone, designed to give pizza dough or bread a nice crust, instead of a tile.

Desserts

Mini Cheesecakes
with Chocolate Curls or Fruit
Jane Collins, Springfield, Ohio

12 Servings

- 2 (8-oz.) packages cream cheese, softened
- ½ cup sugar
- ½ teaspoon vanilla
- 2 eggs
- 12 chocolate sandwich cookies or vanilla wafers

Garnish:

Chocolate curls

Variation: fresh berries or fruit

Preheat oven to 350 F. Beat cream cheese, sugar and vanilla in large bowl with wire whisk until well blended. Add eggs, one at a time, beating after each addition until blended.

Place one cookie in the bottom of each of 12 foil or paper cupcake cups in mini-muffin tin. Fill ⅔ full with batter. Bake 20 minutes or until centers are almost set. Cool and refrigerate 3 hours or overnight.

Top each cheesecake with chocolate curls cut from a candy bar with a vegetable peeler. Or top each cheesecake with berries or small pieces of fresh fruit.

Who says you can't make cheesecake in an RV? If you don't travel with a mixer, use a wire whisk. To soften the cream cheese, use the defrost setting on your microwave.

"Just think of all those women on the Titanic who said, 'No, thank you,' to dessert that night. And for what!"

— *Erma Bombeck*

Desserts

Sandy's Chocolate Cheesecake Muffins

Sandy Lusby, Shediac, New Brunswick

12 Servings

- 1 ¼ cups flour
- 1 cup sugar, divided
- ⅓ cup unsweetened cocoa powder
- ½ teaspoon baking soda
- ¼ teaspoon salt
- ⅔ cup buttermilk
- ¼ cup vegetable oil
- ¼ cup butter or margarine, melted and cooled
- 2 eggs, divided
- 1 ⅛ teaspoons vanilla extract, divided
- ⅓ cup chocolate chips
- 2 (3-oz.) packages cream cheese, room temperature
- ¼ cup slivered almonds

Preheat oven to 375 F. Grease 12 muffin cups.

In large bowl, stir together flour, ¾ cup sugar, cocoa powder, baking soda and salt. In another bowl, stir together buttermilk, oil, melted butter, 1 beaten egg and 1 teaspoon vanilla.

Make a well in center of dry ingredients, add buttermilk mixture and stir just to combine. Stir in chocolate chips. Spoon batter into prepared muffin pans.

In medium bowl, make topping by combining cream cheese, remaining ¼ cup of sugar, remaining egg (lightly beaten) and remaining ⅛ teaspoon vanilla. Stir in almonds. Spoon mixture over chocolate batter in muffin cups and swirl slightly with knife.

Bake 20-25 minutes or until toothpick inserted into center comes out clean. Remove from oven and cool 5 minutes, then serve immediately.

This is excellent, according to Sandy's friends and family.

Crescent-Roll Cream Cheese Bars

Julie Hoy, Langhome, Pennsylvania

12 Bars

- 2 tubes refrigerated crescent rolls
- 2 (8-oz.) packages cream cheese, softened
- 1 ¼ cups sugar
- 1 teaspoon vanilla
- 1 egg, separated
- 1 teaspoon cinnamon

Crescent rolls from the grocery's refrigerator section make the crust for Julie's bars.

Open and lay one tube of crescent rolls in the bottom of a 9x13 baking pan, making sure to seal perforations.

In a bowl, combine the cream cheese, 1 cup sugar, egg yolk and vanilla; mix thoroughly. Pour cream cheese mixture over the layer of crescent roll pastry.

Open and layout second roll of crescent rolls on a piece of waxed paper. Seal all perforations. Place this layer over the cream cheese layer, while peeling off waxed paper.

In a bowl, lightly beat egg white and brush over the top. Combine ¼ cup sugar and cinnamon to sprinkle on top. Bake at 350 F for 25-30 minutes. Cool and store in refrigerator.

"Health food may be good for the conscience but Oreos taste a hell of a lot better."
— *Robert Redford*

Desserts

Ed's Favorite Melt-In-Your-Mouth Fudge Brownies

Ethel Lane, Albuquerque, New Mexico

36 Brownies

- 1 ¼ cups butter, softened
- 4 cups sugar
- 8 eggs
- 2 cups flour
- 1 ¼ cups cocoa powder
- 1 teaspoon salt
- 2 teaspoons vanilla
- 2 cups chopped walnuts

Icing:

- ½ cup butter
- 1 ½ oz. unsweetened chocolate
- 3 cups confectioner's sugar, sifted
- 5 tablespoons milk
- 1 teaspoon vanilla
- Chopped walnuts, if desired

Cream butter with sugar. Add eggs one at a time and beat. Combine flour, cocoa powder and salt; add to mixture and stir to blend. Stir in vanilla and nuts. Spread in greased 15x10x1-inch baking pan. Bake at 325 F for 40-45 minutes. Cool 10 minutes.

Icing: Melt butter and chocolate in saucepan or double boiler. Remove from heat. Add half of confectioner's sugar and blend. Add milk and blend. Add vanilla and remaining sugar. Beat until smooth and spread over warm brownies. Sprinkle with chopped walnuts.

Ethel's recipe makes brownies with a yummy chocolate taste.

"A balanced diet is a cookie in each hand."

— *Barbara Johnson*

Jumbo Three-Chip Cookies
Courtesy of Nestle USA and www.VeryBestBaking.com

24 Cookies

- **4 cups** all-purpose flour
- **1 teaspoon** baking powder
- **1 teaspoon** baking soda
- **1 ½ cups (3 sticks)** butter, softened
- **1 ¼ cups** granulated sugar
- **1 ¼ cups** packed brown sugar
- **2** large eggs
- **1 tablespoon** vanilla extract
- **1 cup (6 oz.)** milk chocolate morsels
- **1 cup (6 oz.)** semi-sweet chocolate morsels
- **½ cup (3 oz.)** white chocolate morsels
- **1** cup chopped nuts

Preheat oven to 375 F. Combine flour, baking powder and baking soda in medium bowl. Beat butter, granulated sugar and brown sugar in large mixer bowl until creamy. Beat in eggs and vanilla extract. Gradually beat in flour mixture. Stir in morsels and nuts.

Drop dough by level ¼ cup measure 2 inches apart onto ungreased baking sheets. Bake for 12 to 14 minutes or until light golden brown. Cool on baking sheets for 2 minutes; remove to wire racks to cool completely.

Using a ¼ cup measuring cup to drop the dough onto the cookie sheet makes these cookies the size of hubcaps!

Desserts

Peanut Butter Cookies

Letha Armstrong, Mansfield, Louisiana

18 Cookies

- 1 cup peanut butter (crunchy or plain)
- 1 cup sugar
- 1 egg

Mix together and roll into small balls. Crisscross them with a fork, like any other peanut butter cookie, and bake at 375 F for 6-8 minutes. Let cool slightly before removing from pan.

Letha says: "This recipe was given to me by a friend and I could not believe it worked — it has only three ingredients."

Chocolate Chess Pie

Pam Hopkins, Louisville, Kentucky

8 Servings

- 1 ½ cups sugar
- 3 ½ tablespoons cocoa
- 1 teaspoon vanilla
- 1 (5-oz.) can evaporated milk
- 2 eggs, beaten
- ¼ pound margarine, melted
- 1 unbaked 9-inch pie shell

Combine all ingredients. Pour into pie shell. Bake at 325 F, 50-55 minutes.

Chess pie is a dessert characteristic of Southern U.S. cuisine. This one is simple to make, using a prepared pie shell and a few simple ingredients you might already have in your RV pantry.

All-American Apricot Lattice Pie

California Fresh Apricot Council

8 Servings

- 1 package refrigerated (not frozen) dough, for 2 pie crusts
- 5 ½ cups sliced fresh apricots, about 2 pounds
- 1 cup sugar
- ¼ cup all-purpose flour
- 2 tablespoons unsalted butter

When roadside stands and farmer's markets offer fresh, tree-ripened fruit, treat your family to this taste-of-summer pie. To ripen firm fruit, place it in a paper bag with an apple or banana.

Preheat oven to 400 F.

On a lightly floured surface, roll the dough into two rounds, each about ⅛-inch thick and 12 inches in diameter. Transfer one crust to a 9- or 10-inch pie pan, and let the extra dough hang over the edge.

In a large bowl, combine the apricots, sugar and flour; toss gently. Pile fruit mixture evenly into pastry-lined pan. Dot with butter.

To make lattice top, cut remaining crust into long strips ½- to ¾-inch wide with a fluted pastry wheel or knife. Use longer strips near the center of the pie and shorter ones near the edges.

Arrange the strips in one direction across the pie and then in the opposite direction.

When all strips are in place, trim the pastry all around with scissors so you have about ½ inch of overhang. Press firmly around the rim to seal the crusts together, then fold the overhang under itself all around to make an upstanding edge. Flute the edge.

Place pie on a foil-lined baking sheet in the oven, reduce heat to 375 F, and bake until crust is golden and juices are bubbling, 50-60 minutes.

Desserts

Mile-High Cranapple-Rhubarb Pie

Mildred Paul, Chattanooga, Tennessee

8 Servings

- 1 Refrigerated crust for 2-crust pie
- 2 cups rhubarb, sliced
- 2 cups Granny Smith apples, peeled and sliced
- 1 ½ cups fresh cranberries
- 1 ¾ cups sugar
- ¾ cup water
- 2 tablespoons all-purpose flour
- 1 tablespoon margarine

Mildred won the Tennessee State Fair Pie Contest with this recipe.

In medium saucepan, cook rhubarb, apples and cranberries in water until cranberries pop. Add sugar, margarine and flour mixed in 2 tablespoons water. Cook until mixture thickens.

Pour into prepared crust. Add top crust. Protect crust edges with foil. Bake at 350 F for approximately 35 minutes.

Grilled Apples for a Quick and Easy Dessert!

Apples can be skewered or baked in a foil packet. Use Granny Smith, Mackintosh or other good cooking apples and cook 10-15 minutes until the outsides are golden (if peeled), or they are tender (use a skewer to test). Sprinkle with cinnamon and brown sugar before wrapping in foil or after skewer-toasting.

Desserts

Handmade Cherry-Almond Pie
Washington State Fruit Commission

8 Servings

- ½ cup sliced almonds, divided
- 1 refrigerated pastry for 9-inch double-crust pie
- 1 egg, beaten
- 4 cups pitted fresh sweet cherries
- ⅓ cup sugar
- 3 tablespoons cornstarch
- 1 teaspoon ground cinnamon
- ¼ teaspoon salt
- 2 tablespoons red wine

Red wine glaze, optional:

- 2 cups powdered sugar mixed with ⅓ cup red wine

No pie pan needed; just put the dough on a baking sheet and wrap the edges around the fruit. The French call this open-face, free-form tart a galette.

Finely chop ¼ cup almonds. Roll dough into a circle approximately 16 inches in diameter (If using packaged pre-rolled pastry, stack one crust on top of the other and roll). Sprinkle chopped almonds over the dough and roll gently to imbed the nuts in the dough. Gently transfer to a lightly greased baking sheet (lined with parchment paper, if desired). Brush with beaten egg.

Mix cherries, sugar, cornstarch, cinnamon, salt and wine. Spoon cherry mixture into dough, leaving a 4-inch border. Lift the edges of the dough up and over the fruit, leaving a 5-inch circle of cherries showing in the center. Fold in the edges of the pastry to form a rough circle.

Brush the pastry with remaining egg, sprinkle with remaining almond slices. Bake at 375 F for 30 minutes until the pastry browns and the filling bubbles. Let stand 15 minutes before cutting. Top with Red Wine Glaze.

Desserts

Old-Fashioned Black Bottom Pie

Carol Reiss, Albertson, New York

8 Servings

- 1   9-inch baked pie shell or graham cracker crust
- 3   tablespoons sugar
- ⅓   cup margarine or butter, melted
- 6   squares semi-sweet baking chocolate, divided
- 2   cups cold milk
- 1   package (4-serving size) vanilla flavor instant pudding and pie filling

Topping:

- 1   cup thawed whipped topping or instant whipped cream
- Chocolate curls

Place margarine and four of the chocolate squares in a small saucepan; cook on MEDIUM heat until chocolate is completely melted and mixture is well blended, stirring frequently. Spread onto bottom of crust; set aside.

Pour milk into medium bowl. Add dry pudding mix. Beat with wire whisk 2 minutes or until well blended. Pour into crust. Refrigerate at least 1 hour or until ready to serve.

Meanwhile, use remaining 2 chocolate squares to make chocolate curls, using a vegetable peeler. Refrigerate until ready to use. Top pie with whipped topping and chocolate curls just before serving.

Carson Gulley, who grew up in a big family on an Arkansas farm, worked his way up from dishwasher to head chef at the University of Wisconsin residence hall in Madison, where he invented the black bottom pie — still the university's signature dish.

Carol's version is a real treat, too.

"There are four basic food groups: milk chocolate, dark chocolate, white chocolate and chocolate truffles."

— *Unknown*

Desserts

Chocolate Truffle Cream Pie

Candy Raffaele, Alamogordo, New Mexico

8 Servings

- **2** bars (4-oz. each) milk chocolate, broken into pieces
- **1** cup pecan pieces
- **1** cup whipping cream
- **3** tablespoons dark chocolate liqueur

Garnish:
> **Whipped cream**
>
> **Grated milk chocolate**

Combine half (1 bar) of broken chocolate and pecans in bowl of food processor or blender. Process until crumbly. Press crumbs into 8-inch pie plate or 4 custard cups.

In a small saucepan, melt remaining chocolate with cream on LOW heat, stirring constantly until smooth. (Do not boil.) Add chocolate liqueur. Chill in the pan at least 2 hours or until very cold. Beat until thick and creamy. Spread into crust. Chill 1 hour. Garnish with whipped cream and grated chocolate, if desired.

You can prepare the chocolate-and-pecan crumbs before leaving home if you don't take a blender or food processor on RV trips.

Oh! Peanut Butter S'more Empanadas

Spread about 3 tablespoons of plain or crunchy peanut butter over half of an 8 to 10-inch flour tortilla. Top with some tiny marshmallows, semisweet chocolate chips and sliced banana. Fold tortillas in half, pressing gently to flatten and seal slightly. Grill in a wire basket or directly on the grill, turning once, until tortillas are golden. Cut each empanada into 4 wedges.

Desserts

Classic Chocolate Mayonnaise Cake

S. Weintz, Las Vegas, Nevada

9 Servings

- 2 cups sifted all-purpose flour
- 1 teaspoon baking powder
- 1 teaspoon baking soda
- ½ teaspoon salt
- ¼ cup cocoa powder
- ¾ cup mayonnaise
- 1 cup sugar
- 1 cup water
- 1 teaspoon vanilla

This ultra-moist chocolate cake is always a big hit. Just don't tell them you used mayonnaise … unless you want the cake all to yourself.

Preheat oven to 350 F. Grease a 9-inch square cake pan.

In one bowl, sift together first 5 ingredients (flour, baking powder, baking soda, salt and cocoa powder). Set aside.

Combine mayonnaise and sugar in a separate bowl. Blend until smooth.

Add the dry ingredients alternately with the water and the vanilla to ensure even mixing. Beat until smooth. Spoon into the greased 9-inch square pan.

Bake for 35 minutes or until done. The top should spring back when lightly touched. Do not over-bake.

Desserts

Self-Frosting Chocolate Zucchini Cake

Bill Coulter, Helena, Montana

12 Servings

- ½ cup margarine
- ½ cup oil
- 1 ¾ cups sugar
- 2 eggs
- 1 teaspoon vanilla
- 2 ½ cups flour
- 1 teaspoon baking soda
- 1 teaspoon salt
- 5 tablespoons cocoa
- ½ cup sour milk (or ½ cup milk plus 2 teaspoons vinegar)
- 2 cups finely grated zucchini
- 2 cups mini chocolate chips
- ¾ cup finely chopped nuts
- ¾ cup brown sugar

Mix oil, margarine and sugar together in a bowl. Add eggs and vanilla.

Sift flour and remaining dry ingredients together, add to sugar mixture alternately with milk. Blend well. Stir in zucchini by hand.

Pour batter into a 9x13 pan. Mix together chocolate chips, brown sugar and nuts. Crumble evenly over top of cake batter. Bake at 350 F for 40-45 minutes.

No icing to mix — but, sadly, no bowl to lick!

"Vegetables are a must on a diet. I suggest carrot cake, zucchini bread and pumpkin pie."

— Jim Davis, "Garfield"

Desserts

Black Forest Cobbler

Debbie Guy, Hattiesburg, Mississippi

8 Servings

- 1 (¼ pound) stick butter or margarine, sliced in pieces
- 1 box devil's food or chocolate cake mix
- 1 can cherry-pie filling

Place entire stick of butter pieces in bottom of 14-inch Dutch oven or skillet.

In a separate bowl add all other ingredients listed for the cake mix, except eggs. Mix cake thoroughly by hand. Pour cake mix into dutch oven or skillet on top of butter pieces. Spoon cherry-pie filling on top of cake mix.

Bake at the time and temperature suggested on the cake-mix box (about 25 minutes).

Debbie describes this cake as heavy, more like brownies. The cherries end up on the bottom, and when they smell it baking, neighbors from miles around will come to check on what you are fixing!

> *"I don't think a really good pie can be made without a dozen or so children peeking over your shoulder as you stoop to look in at it every little while."*
>
> — *John Gould*

Desserts

Cherry Pineapple Delight

Lee Smith, Lakehills, Texas

12 Servings

- 1 **package yellow cake mix**
- 1 **can cherry pie filling**
- 1 **(20-oz.) can crushed pineapple**
- 1 **cup flaked or shredded coconut**
- 1 **cup chopped pecans**
- ¾ **cup (1 ½ sticks) butter**

Here's a typical "dump cake" recipe that's really simple and will satisfy everyone's sweet tooth.

Line 9x13 pan with aluminum foil. Pour in and mix cherry pie filling and pineapple. Sprinkle cake mix over mixture. Sprinkle coconut and pecans over cake mix. Melt butter and pour over the top. Bake at 350 F for 45 (or so) minutes, until top is golden and filling is bubbling.

Rock-n-Roll Ice Cream

Joan Lynch, Wesley Chapel, Florida

4 Servings

- 1 **3-pound empty coffee can and plastic lid, cleaned**
- 1 **1-pound empty coffee can and plastic lid, cleaned**
- 1 **pint (2 cups) half-and-half**
- ½ **cup sugar**
- 1 **teaspoon vanilla**
- 1 **tablespoon chocolate syrup or a few pieces of frozen fruit**

  Ice and rock salt

In the smaller can, mix the half-and-half with the sugar. Add vanilla and chocolate syrup or frozen fruit. Cover the small can with its lid. Put the small can inside the larger can. Add ice to cover the small can. Sprinkle about 2 tablespoons rock salt over the ice. Secure the lid on the larger can.

On a flat surface, roll the can back and forth with your hands and/or feet, Check in about 10 minutes to see if the ice cream is hard enough. If not, replace the lids and continue to roll a while longer.

Who needs an ice-cream maker when you have some energetic children? They'll love making it!

Desserts

Ford's Eggless Cake
Ford Marshall, Calgary, Alberta

6 Servings

- 1 ½ cups flour
- 4 tablespoons cocoa powder
- 1 teaspoon baking soda
- 1 cup sugar
- ½ teaspoon salt
- 1 tablespoon white vinegar
- 5 tablespoons canola oil
- 1 ½ teaspoons vanilla
- 1 cup cold water

Sift or stir dry ingredients together in an ungreased 8-inch square or round pan. Mix well. Make 3 wells. In these put vinegar, oil and vanilla. Pour water all over and mix till well blended. Bake at 350 F for 35 minutes. Use your favorite topping or none at all.

This wacky cake can be mixed in an 8-inch ungreased pan using just a fork. Mixes and bakes within an hour. You can double the recipe with ease for a two-layer cake.

"You can say this for ready-mixes — the next generation isn't going to have any trouble making pies exactly like mother used to make."

— *Earl Wilson*

Desserts

Dinner for Man's Best Friend!

Flo's Favorite Dog Food, page 186

Home-Made Dog Food

John Crean and Barbara Venezia, Riverside, California
(John Crean is the former CEO and chairman of Fleetwood Enterprises Inc.)

Meals for Days

- 4 cups of uncooked instant rice
- 2 large carrots
- 4 potatoes
- Rubber cooking gloves
- 3 pounds of 30% fat hamburger
- 4 eggs
- ¼ cup of wheat germ
- 1 pound of cooked navy beans
- 4 teaspoons of beef bouillon
- 1 teaspoon of salt

This is the most-requested recipe from *At Home On the Range: The Cooking Show for the Deranged.*

Cook instant rice per package instructions. In a food processor, shred the carrots and potatoes. Mix them together in a very large bowl.

Here's where your rubber cooking gloves come in handy. After you've put on your protective covering, add in the meat, eggs, wheat germ, cooked navy beans, cooked rice, bouillon and salt. Mush this with your hands until there are no lumps in the mixture.

Now, take a large baking pan and place the mixture in the pan. Bake in the oven for about 1 ½ hours at a temperature of 350 F.

Serve at room temperature. This can be refrigerated and served to your dog for up to two weeks. If your pooch is a gourmet, you might want to garnish this with parsley. This can also be served to your mother-in-law with catsup!

"To his dog, every man is Napoleon."

— Aldous Huxley

In addition to recipe and photo sources indicated in each chapter, photos were also provided by:

© iStockphoto.com

rarpia, James McQuillan, Anthony Hall, Karen Grotzinger, Jamie Travis, Louis Aguindldo, Rohit Seth, Lori Sparkla, Christine Balderas, Irene Teesalu, Johanna Goodyear, Yanik Chauvin, Greg Nicholas, gwmullis, eyecrave, José Carlos Piers Pereira, Stephen Walls, Dan Brandenburg, Rasmus Rasmussen, Kelly Cline, Michael Gatewood, Rob Friedman, blaneyphoto, Paul Cowan, Cameron Pashak, angelafoto, Roberto Adrian, Lisa F. Young, Jason Stitt, creacart, boomzfoto, Zoran Mercetic, Liv Friis-Larsen, Duncan Babbage.

National Cattlemen's Beef Association, www.beefitswhatsfordinner.com

National Pork Board, www.theotherwhitemeat.com

National Watermelon Promotion Board, www.watermelon.org

United States Potato Board, www.potatohelp.com

Robert George, Direct Design

Photo Credits

Notes

Notes

Notes